Dürer and his Time

136. WOLF HUBER: Crucifixion

Dürer and his Time

AN EXHIBITION FROM THE COLLECTION OF
THE PRINT ROOM, STATE MUSEUM, BERLIN
STIFTUNG PREUSSISCHER KULTURBESITZ

CATALOGUE AND NOTES BY
FEDJA ANZELEWSKI

SMITHSONIAN PRESS, WASHINGTON, D.C. 1967

SMITHSONIAN PUBLICATION 4647 · ORIGINALLY ISSUED 1965 BY THE
SMITHSONIAN INSTITUTION TRAVELING EXHIBITION SERVICE
PRODUCED BY THE MERIDEN GRAVURE COMPANY
AND THE ANTHOENSEN PRESS
DESIGNED BY CRIMILDA PONTES

Acknowledgments

The exhibition "Dürer and His Time" represents one of the greatest periods of draftsmanship the world has known. Few eras have equaled the diversity, refinement, and expression of German graphic art between 1470 and 1530. Albrecht Dürer himself stands out not only as the supreme master of line but also as the genius who united the Gothic spirit with the Renaissance. We are fortunate that the Stiftung Preussischer Kulturbesitz in Berlin, whose Print Room in the Staatliche Museen contains one of the world's greatest collections of drawings, graciously consented to share with the American public the treasures entrusted to their care.

To Dr. Hans Möhle, Director of the Print Room, go our deepest thanks for the good will and zeal that made the loan possible. We are deeply indebted to Dr. Fedja Anzelewski for his scholarly catalogue and dedication to the exhibition's purpose. Both the German Foreign Office and the United States Department of State lent support to the project, and His Excellency, Heinrich Knappstein, the German Ambassador, has generously agreed to sponsor the exhibition while it is in the United States.

The present exhibition was first prepared for showings in Brussels and Amsterdam in 1964-65. We are grateful to Dr. J. Van Lerberghe, Conseiller of the Ministère de l'Instruction Publique in Brussels, for his cooperation during the preliminary stages of negotiation.

The Republic of Germany sends many exhibitions abroad in its program of cultural exchange to further international understanding. It is indeed an honor for the Smithsonian Institution to bring to the United States the latest and most splendid exhibition of the series, "Dürer and His Time."

The catalogue was translated from the French by Mrs. Benita Eisler and was edited by Mr. Thomas C. Witherspoon of the Smithsonian Press. The loan, and tour to the National Gallery of Art, The Pierpont Morgan Library, The Art Institute of Chicago, and The Museum of Fine Arts (Boston) were arranged by the Smithsonian Institution Traveling Exhibition Service, with the special attention of Mrs. Dorothy Van Arsdale and Mrs. Michael Padnos. Warmest thanks are also due to Mrs. Erika Passantino for her work on the catalogue.

S. DILLON RIPLEY, *Secretary*
Smithsonian Institution

The Print Room of the Berlin Museum and its Collections of 16th century German Master Drawings

Of the great European collections of prints and drawings, the Print Room of the Berlin Museum is the youngest. Those of Vienna, Paris, and London were all formed at an earlier period, which accounts for the importance and extent of their treasures. The Berlin collection owes its creation to Friedrich-Wilhelm III of Prussia, but a much more important role in its formation was played by Baron von Humboldt (1767-1835), the famous scientist, statesman, friend of Goethe and Schiller, and founder of the University of Berlin. In fact, von Humboldt and Carl Friedrich von Rumohr (1785-1843) must be considered the key figures in the beginnings of the Print Room.

It is worth noting that only a small part of the Berlin art collections is of royal provenance. Unlike many European or German dynasties, the House of Prussia-Brandenburg had only a minor interest in art collecting, whereas the museums of Vienna, Dresden, and Munich, notably, owe the wealth and scope of their treasures primarily to the Hapsburgs of Wettin and Wittelsbach. Acquisitions made by these museums since the end of the nineteenth century are of considerably less importance than the initial royal contributions. But the reverse is true of Berlin. The Berlin Museums are important worldwide because in the nineteenth century and, above all, in the course of the last hundred years the core which existed at the outset has been supplemented by acquisitions made in a systematic fashion by applying, from the very beginning, the methods of art history.

The collections of master drawings in the Print Room cover four centuries, from the late 1400's to 1900, and now include more than 22,000 works. The royal collection, opened to the public in 1831, occupied a section of the first museum, built in 1830 by Carl Friedrich Schinkel and located in the castle park. This collection consisted of no more than 500 drawings, most of them originally owned by the Elector Friedrich-Wilhelm von Brandenburg (1620-88). His small collection of drawings was purchased from the painter Matthäus Merian the Younger, son of the renowned topographer Matthäus Merian the Elder. Although the great German masters Dürer, Grünewald, and Hans Holbein the Younger were not represented in this collection, there were many works by Hans Holbein the Elder, Lucas Cranach the Elder, Hans Baldung Grien, Hans Schäufelein, Albrecht Altdorfer, and the Housebook Master, as well as drawings by Rubens and van Dyck. Still, the new Print Room played a small role in the European art world when compared to similar institutions. The acquisition of a distinguished but small collection of prints belonging to Captain von Derschau of Nuremberg and others given by Counts Corneillan and Lepell shortly before 1831 scarcely changed matters. When von Humboldt purchased the collection of von Nagler (the Postal Director and Minister of State) in 1835, however, the Berlin Print Room assumed a place among the most important institutions of its kind in Europe.

The von Nagler collection in its day was the richest private assemblage of graphic art in Germany, noted as much for its variety as for its abundance of masterpieces in the areas of drawings, prints, old illustrated books, and medieval illuminated manuscripts. With its acquisition many thousands of items were added to the Berlin Print Room. Notable among these were precious old master drawings of all the European schools, including seventy-five in silverpoint by Hans Holbein the Elder, once attributed to Dürer, and today considered major documents of the art of the portrait in Germany.

With the original space allotted to the Print Room rapidly becoming insufficient, the collections of graphic art were transferred in 1839-40 to the castle of Monbijou on the River Spree. These new quarters in turn became too restricted, and in 1848 the Print Room was moved to a new building, designed by Friedrich August Stüler, close to Schinkel's old museum. There in spacious and well-proportioned rooms on the third floor the collections of prints and drawings were housed next to the Egyptian and Greco-Roman antiquities. During 1943-44 this building was destroyed. The ruins still stand amid Berlin's "Island of Museums" and there are no plans for reconstruction in the immediate future.

The golden age of the Berlin Print Room was between 1870 and the beginnings of the Nazi regime in 1933. This was the era of Wilhelm von Bode, the veritable creator of the Berlin Museums, who was from 1872 to 1929 assistant director, director, and finally director general. Although he was never directly in charge of the Print Room, it is nonetheless due to his initiative and erudition that 400 drawings of incomparable value were acquired in 1874 from the collection of Berthold Suermondt of Aachen. This collection contained numerous drawings by outstanding German masters. Again thanks to von Bode, the Print Room was further enriched

8

one year later by the collection of the chief architect of Hanover, Berthold Haus-man, which contained numerous important German master drawings.

In 1876 Friederich Lippmann was named Director of the Berlin Print Room. Erudition joined with intellectual curiosity and organizational ability made Lippmann a man of many talents. He classified and catalogued the ever-growing collections, and this most fruitful of his activities resulted in making the Print Room available to a large public as well as useful to specialists—comparable in this respect to the British Museum. The system of classification which Lippmann established was so satisfactory that it is still in use today; it was under his directorship as well that the first serious studies appeared in the field of drawings. Through his innumerable purchases of exceptional works—both single and group acquisitions—Lippmann established areas of specialization within the Print Room's collections: the graphic art of Martin Schongauer, the precursors of Dürer, Dürer himself, and Rembrandt. At the same time he raised the collection of German masters to a level unequaled anywhere in the world. To give but one example, the purchase of the Viennese Posanyi-Hulot collection in 1877 brought no less than forty drawings by Albrecht Dürer into the Print Room. Others followed shortly thereafter. (There is no doubt that a few of these drawings had been in the Albertina a century earlier. This royal collection of fabulous treasures could boast in 1783 of possessing 371 Dürer drawings acquired by the Emperor Rudolph II of Prague at the death of Willibald Imhoff. The 150 of these drawings still owned by the Albertina constitute the most important group of Dürer drawings anywhere.)

If under Lippmann's directorship the Berlin collection of Dürer drawings acquired worldwide renown, the talents of Max J. Friedländer, director from 1908 to 1929, and Friedrich Winkler, director from 1933 to 1957, brought new scope to the collection in both quality and quantity. Friedländer enriched the collection with sixteen drawings and Winkler with a dozen. Included among the latter are the best and most important examples of Dürer's draftsmanship. No other collector, however astute, could have succeeded in discovering, selecting, and acquiring them as Winkler did. His personality combined passion, knowledge, and scholarship to the great gain of the museum. This happy fusion of qualities was, moreover, to be found in several curators of the Berlin Museums after Wilhelm von Bode. Under von Bode and his successors the complex of the Berlin Museums grew to embrace nineteen different sections and became one of the principal research centers for the history of art. Friedländer, an outstanding connoisseur of early Netherlandish art, was also a great Dürer scholar. Under his direction and with the help of Elfried Bock and Jakob Rosenberg, associate curators, two critical catalogues of German and Netherlandish drawings were published. As for Friedrich Winkler, he was justly considered a foremost specialist on and historiographer of Dürer.

While the 130 Dürer drawings in the Berlin Print Room remain inferior in number to those of the Albertina, they surpass them in scope. The complete evolution of the great draftsman's style is represented in the Berlin collection, from early drawings done at the age of thirteen (cat. 17) to the last works of his full maturity (cat. 55, 56) and including masterpieces exemplifying his different techniques. Only one third of this collection is represented in the present exhibition.

Dürer is not the only artist who demonstrates the spirit of German master drawings, although he is its most renowned spokesman and representative. In temperament as well as style he stands between two poles: on the one hand the visionary art of Grünewald, with its startling images inspired by medieval mysticism, and on the other the spare and rigorous linear style of Hans Holbein the Younger, with its classical vocabulary.

To penetrate the extraordinary and impassioned art of Matthias Grünewald—the image of an almost unfathomable German mind and sensibility—one must visit the Print Room of the Berlin-Dahlem Museum as well as see the Isenheim Altar at Colmar. Of the thirty-six absolutely authentic drawings by Grünewald known to exist, nineteen are to be found in the Berlin Print Room, five in East Berlin, and fourteen in West Berlin. In 1925 Friedländer discovered and purchased for the Print Room seven of the best drawings of a then unknown series by Grünewald that formed part of the collection of a family of Frankfurt jurists, the von Savignys. Two other Grünewald drawings were purchased by Winkler in 1936 from the Ehlers collection. In 1952 three more by the same master were discovered in East Berlin. The last five of these drawings are now in the Print Room of the East Berlin Museum. The other Grünewald drawings in the Berlin Print Room were part of the original collection. Taken as a group the Dürer and Grünewald drawings in the Berlin collections constitute the pinnacle of German master drawings and are recognized as masterpieces the world over.

The last of these three great German draftsmen, Hans Holbein the Younger, of Augsburg, part of whose artistic activity took place in Basel and London, can be thoroughly studied only in the Print Room of Basel and at Windsor Castle, although of the nine Holbein drawings in Berlin five are of exceptionally high quality. Furthermore, the seventy-five silverpoint drawings by Hans Holbein the Elder in the Berlin collections are a unique treasure. Taken from several different sketchbooks, these pages show the human face unadorned, most notably in portraits of Augsburg sitters. Here the work of the father is seen as the prototype of the brilliant draftsmanship of the son.

That extraordinary era, the century of Dürer, so rich in creative genius, finds its most faithful reflection in the Berlin Print Room. Besides the trinity of Dürer, Grünewald, and Holbein, two other great artists of the romantic era, Albrecht Altdorfer and Wolf Huber of the Danube School, are respectively represented in Berlin by twenty and eighteen drawings of uncontested attribution. Undoubtedly the most gifted pupil of Dürer was Hans Baldung Grien. The Print Room possesses twenty original drawings by this artist.

Fortunately, this rich collection of German master drawings survived World War II without loss. When danger from air attack became imminent the collection was transferred elsewhere in Berlin for safekeeping. In 1945 it was moved to a mine in central Germany, joining a group that had been sent there earlier. From there the collection was taken by the U. S. Army of Occupation to the Landesmuseum in Wiesbaden, remaining there until it was reinstalled in the Berlin-Dahlem Museum in 1956-57. This museum, located in the university sector of West Berlin, was conceived before World War I by Wilhelm von Bode as a museum of Asian art. Left unfinished since 1918, it was rebuilt in 1950 to house the recovered treasures of the Berlin Museum.

The Print Room, whose collection is at least four fifths of its prewar size, has only temporary housing. Today its treasures are once again accessible to the public in a small study room and a single inadequate exhibition room. The Stiftung Preussischer Kulturbesitz, in which the different states of the Federal Republic are represented, was formed some years ago as a high council for the Berlin Museums. This institution has planned the construction of a new museum and graphic art center to house the Print Room near the Tiergarten among the new Philharmonic Hall of Berlin, the Gallery of 20th-Century Art, and the State Library.

DR. HANS MÖHLE
Director of the Print Room

Notes on Drawing at the Time of Dürer

The years from 1470 to 1530, which represent the golden age of German painting, coincide almost exactly with Dürer's lifetime. The three generations marking the artistic life of this period can, to an extraordinary degree, be designated by the names of the three most important artists: Martin Schongauer, Albrecht Dürer, and Hans Holbein the Younger; and Dürer is considered by all the central figure of his time. His fame rests upon his drawings; through them he surpassed all of his contemporaries. Nevertheless, many other artists who worked in his shadow were remarkable draftsmen. Indeed, German art is more distinguished for its draftsmen than for its great painters.

Drawing is certainly the most original and spontaneous means of expression of all the visual arts. In general it reflects the artist's aspirations with much more fidelity than does a painting, which usually is elaborately planned down to its most minute details. The draftsman is not obliged to take into account the desires of a donor; he is his own master. Thus the "handwriting" of an artist is freely expressed in a drawing. This spontaneity of artistic expression very early prompted art lovers to collect drawings (the oldest collections date from about 1500). More than any other art form drawings throw light upon the creative process and upon the genesis of a work of art. When the circumstances are favorable all the phases of a major work can be traced through master drawings, from the first rapid sketch, where an idea is gradually established, through the study of details that develop and enlighten this idea, to its definitive form.

In European art of the modern era the drawing has an essentially preparatory role, one conditioned by contemporary opinion which requires that, for a given theme, a painter must find forms that are original, independent, and different, if possible, from all previous versions. This point of view is in direct opposition to that of the medieval artist, for whom the content of a subject had more importance than the process of creation itself. Until the fifteenth century, painters had generally remained close to preceding examples. The detailed, drawn study was not indispensable, since each painter, or at least each workshop, had a sufficient number of models at its disposal. These have survived in the form of model books.

In the fifteenth century a profound change took place. Great painters such as Masaccio, the van Eycks, and Hugo van der Goes created new forms and new compositions. Nevertheless, if one considers the few drawings by these artists known to exist, they would not appear to have carried on their experiments in detail by means of drawings. It was only in the fifteenth century that drawings multiplied all over Europe. And from 1500 on the art of drawing followed an unbroken course.

German drawings occupy a special place in this period. Those which survive are in many ways more important than those of other European countries, with the possible exception of Italy. This is probably not due to chance preservation but rather to the markedly pronounced affinity of German artists for the graphic arts.

The fundamental means of expression of all graphic art is line, which within nature is an element imperceptible to the senses. In German art, much more than in any other school, linear art became the established mode of expression, and to an eye accustomed to the drawings of Raphael or Rubens, the creations of German art often seem disturbing. Even in Dürer the expressive line plays a much greater role than in the work of his contemporaries in the Netherlands. By his mastery of technique Dürer was able to integrate this means of expression within a graphic system that facilitates the comprehension of the viewer without his even being aware of the importance of line.

Immediately related to the predominantly expressive character of line is another peculiarity of German drawing that must be taken into consideration: the visible and frequent absence of harmony and beauty as defined by the classical concept. The dominant tendency of German artists of all times is in the direction of the particular and individual, much more than toward the general or ideal aspect of things. A third characteristic derives from the drawing constituting a finished work when carried to its most detailed state. These German drawings are autonomous works of art, destined for no other end than to be sold or given away in the same manner as any other artistic creation. A painting by Dürer after one of these meticulously finished drawings has yet to be discovered (cat. 38). The two charcoal portraits by Dürer (cat. 30 and 41) also belong to the category of autonomous drawings.

The drawing by the Master of the Stötteritz Altar (cat. 9) and the pen drawing of *Christ on the Mount of Olives* by Hans Burgkmair (cat. 112) should be considered as studies for altarpieces. In Lucas Cranach's sketch for a polyptych, the preparatory work is already quite advanced. A pen and ink drawing representing a scene from the life of St. Paul (cat. 95) by Hans Holbein the Elder is, to all appearances, a preparatory study for a painting. The *Parnassus* of Hans Holbein the Younger (cat. 111) constitutes the first stage of a project for a festival decor, the completed design for which has been lost.

Every stage, from the first preparatory sketch to the definitive drawing, may be followed in studies for stained glass windows. This evolution moves from a small notation by Hans von Kulmbach for a detail of the Emperor's window in the choir of the Church of St. Sebaldus in Nuremberg (cat. 72) to the portrait, with its magnificent purity of line, of the abbot of the Monastery of St. Egidius (cat. 71), or again, the study for a window by Hans Holbein the Younger (cat. 110). In the *Massacre of the Innocents* by Sebald Beham (cat. 78) one can still see the red chalk outlines which the glassmaker drew as a tracing before cutting the glass.

In the fifteenth and sixteenth centuries painters were frequently commissioned to create projects for sculpture or metalwork or to design ornamental motifs to be engraved on armor. The *Martyrdom of Holy Knights* by Niklaus Manuel Deutsch (cat. 146) is a characteristic example of a study for sculpture. The little ornament drawing by Dürer (cat. 44), the design by Urs Graf for a dagger sheath (cat. 143), and the drawing by Peter Flötner for a dagger (cat. 81) were all destined for goldsmiths.

Using drawings from nature for the elaboration of certain details is the final stage in the preparation of a work of art. Dürer gives us characteristic examples with his drawings for the *Feast of the Rose Garlands*, a painting destined for the German Merchants' Chapel in Venice (cat. 35), and for the Heller Altar (cat. 37) in the Dominican Church in Frankfurt. Also in this category is the *Kneeling Virgin* by Grünewald, a study for an Annunciation (cat. 60).

Not all of these drawings were created for a specific purpose. Dürer frequently borrowed from documentary drawings he had done previously, using them as models for paintings, woodcuts, or engravings, depending on the project at hand. The importance accorded to their drawings by German artists is proved by the appearance at the end of the fifteenth century of signatures and dates. Dürer, who recognized his own talent at an early age, seems to have set the example. His *Virgin Enthroned, with the Infant Christ and Two Angel Musicians* (cat. 17), dating from 1485, is one of the oldest signed and dated drawings. The signature in the form of a monogram affixed to every finished drawing became the most usual form in the sixteenth century.

Writing in his family chronicle, Albrecht Dürer noted: "Then Albrecht Dürer, my dear father, came to Germany, having for a long time remained in the Lowlands, where he had become acquainted with great artists. . . ." This note acquires

15

its full significance when we learn that at that period numerous German painters and goldsmiths flocked to the Netherlands. They were following, by going to the source, the progress of an art which was in full flower at the sumptuous court of the Dukes of Burgundy and in their opulent cities. Hans Memling of Seligenstadt even became a Flemish subject, while Erhard Reuwich of Utrecht, the Housebook Master, can be considered a Rhenish artist.

With Martin Schongauer, German art may be said to have reached its peak, finding its equilibrium through the assimilation of Flemish realism. This most important German painter of the fifteenth century came from a patrician family of Augsburg goldsmiths who had settled in Colmar about 1440. The drawing in the Louvre of the *Judgment of Christ*, to which Dürer later added the date of 1469, proves that Schongauer must have seen the van der Weyden altarpiece in the Hospital of Beaune. But of all Flemish painters, it was Roger who made the strongest impression upon Schongauer and his contemporaries. The elegance of his figures and the expressive quality of his drawing are close to the spirit of Schongauer, whose style clearly unites Roger's influence to the graceful beauty characteristic of the artistic sensibility of the Upper Rhine. As a copper engraver—an activity dear to the son of a goldsmith—Schongauer very soon enjoyed great renown even outside Germany. The purity of his drawings makes us prone to forget that he was also the creator of monumental works of art. The fresco of the *Last Judgment* in the Cathedral of Breisach is proof of this. Soon after the completion of this work the artist died in the same city in 1491.

The Housebook Master is the second great figure of German art of this period. He owes his name to a manuscript illustrated with pen and ink drawings whose text contains precepts and rules of conduct for a Master of Arms. (This work belongs to the collection of Prince Waldburg-Wolfegg.) Old texts give this artist's name as the Master of the Amsterdam Cabinet, for most of his drypoints, of which in many cases only one proof survives, are in Amsterdam. Using stylistic comparisons certain writers have also attributed to him woodcuts for the travel book *Peregrinationes in terram sanctam* by Bernhard von Breydenbach, printed in Mainz in 1486. The narrative itself mentions the Utrecht painter, Erhard Reuwich, the traveling companion of the book's author and printer. Since Erhard is previously mentioned in Mainz, it would be logical to suppose that he is identical to the Housebook Master. With their supple linear style, the Housebook Master's drawings are easily distinguishable from those of his contemporaries. He is modern in spirit, both in his compositions and his themes. Because we can discern the influence of Flemish miniatures in the drawing *A Prince at Table* in Bruges (cat. 7), we can identify the artist who portrayed this historic occasion with Reuwich. We know also that Reuwich left the Netherlands to come to Germany and that his drawings and wood engravings reveal a similar concern with portraying actuality.

The essentially different point of view which distinguishes the Housebook Master (Erhard Reuwich) from his contemporaries is clearly evident when we compare his works with the woodcuts of Dürer or Michael Wolgemut. The latter's woodcuts in the *World Chronicle* by Hartmann Schedel, the Nuremberg humanist and physician, for example, make no reference to contemporary events. All of these illustrations are drawn from imagination and not reality, even though they strongly reveal the imprint of Flemish realism. They were to have a great influence on the stylistic development of the young Dürer. The woodcuts show that Wolgemut was a somewhat crude but highly inventive artist. His compositions often exaggerate the movements of drapery, a mannerism dear to late Gothic art. The only authenticated drawing by his hand is a study, now in London, for the title page of the *World Chronicle*. A Berlin drawing (cat. 10) doubtless by Wolgemut shows the influence of Flemish painting and Schongauer. In his style Wolgemut is close to the drawing of the famed Nuremberg sculptor Veit Stoss (cat. 11).

Three views of Bamberg (cat. 12-14) attributed to Wolfgang Katzheimer may be considered as the immediate antecedents of Dürer's watercolor landscapes. Katzheimer worked as painter to the Bishops of Bamberg, and we can infer from this that he must have been the most noted artist of that city at the end of the fifteenth century and doubtless received commissions for large nature studies.

Among the works by anonymous artists that show some Netherlandish influence, the drawing by the Master of the Drapery Studies (cat. 15) deserves particular attention. It is part of a notebook whose other sheets, all studies of drapery, are now in Berlin and in several other collections. Some scholars have attempted to group a considerable number of other drawings around these sketches. It is evident, however, that not all of these other drawings are the work of a single master but are more likely by several different draftsmen in the upper Rhine region. Some have been recently attributed to the painter and glass designer Peter Hemmel, who was active in Strasburg from 1447 to 1505 (cf. Anzelewsky in *Zeitschrift des deutschen Vereins für Kunstwissenschaft, 1964*), while another group seems to be by the hand of an imitator of the Housebook Master. Our drawing appears closer to the work of Hemmel.

A passage from the *Elementa Rhetorices* (Wittenberg, 1531) by Philip Melanchthon reveals the judgments and esteem accorded the German artists of the sixteenth century by their contemporaries. The humanist qualifies Dürer's style by the term "grandiose" (grandiosa) and the work of Cranach by "graceful" (graciles), while Grünewald is placed somewhere between these two aesthetic tendencies.

Thus did the Wittenberg theologian and friend of Dürer evaluate with a sureness of taste the three most important artists of his time.

Albrecht Dürer was the third of a family of eighteen children born to Albrecht Dürer, a goldsmith who had left Hungary to settle in Germany, and Barbara Holper, a native of Nuremberg. Dürer the Elder taught his son the basic techniques of the goldsmith's craft, but at the age of thirteen Dürer had already decided to become a painter. As he could not become an apprentice to Martin Schongauer, he entered the workshop of his neighbor, Michael Wolgemut. From his father Dürer had already learned the technique of engraving, later to become one of his principal activities. Under Wolgemut's tutelage he studied painting and woodcut illustration. Then in 1490 he left his home as a journeyman, as every artist of the time was obliged to do. The second stage of this trip brought him to Colmar in 1492. There he met only the two brothers of Martin Schongauer, for the latter had died the year before in Breisach. In the beginning of 1494 Dürer was called home by his brother, and soon after his return he married Agnes Frey. That autumn he once again set forth, this time for Venice, returning to Nuremberg in the early part of 1495. From then on paintings, engravings, and woodcuts were produced unceasingly by his inexhaustible genius. The series of woodcuts for the *Apocalypse* and his first engravings immediately assured the fame of the young artist—not yet thirty at the time—in artistic and humanist circles. Between 1505 and 1507 we find him once again in Venice. It was during this sojourn that he painted his greatest altarpiece, the *Feast of the Rose Garlands*, for the German Merchants Chapel. It is now in Prague. When he returned to Germany in 1508 he was commissioned by Jacob Heller, a Frankfurt merchant, to paint an Assumption for an altarpiece. This painting was destroyed by fire in the seventeenth century. The loss was all the more tragic as Grünewald had added two wings to this work in 1511 which are still in existence.

During the meeting of the Diet of Worms in 1518 Dürer went to Augsburg, where he made a portrait drawing of Emperor Maximilian. Then in 1520, accompanied by his wife and a servant, he made a trip through the Netherlands. In Antwerp, a city which he visited frequently, he was held in the highest esteem by his fellow artists. The years following his return to Germany were devoted to his art and particularly to the preparation of his writings on art: *Treatise on Geometry*, *Treatise on Fortification*, and *Four Books on Human Proportions*. The first two treatises were published in 1525 and 1527, while the books on proportion were only published after his death on April 6, 1528.

It would be impossible to overestimate Dürer's place in the art of his time. Through his genius as an engraver he became, in the true sense of the word, the *praeceptor Germaniae*. Further, he greatly influenced Flemish and Italian artists, who looked to him above all for their engraving technique. The technical perfection underlying his form is essentially the fruit of his genius as a draftsman. Each influenced the other to assure his originality and fame.

Dürer possessed absolute mastery of every technique and every means of expression in the realm of drawing. Besides using silverpoint and pen and ink, which were already in use in the Middle Ages, he employed brush, chalk, and charcoal with equal brilliance. In Dürer, diversity of technique corresponded to an astounding flexibility in his means of expression. From the most rapid and spontaneous sketch to the most carefully finished detail or autonomous drawing Dürer utilized the technique and expressive form corresponding to the nature of the particular drawing. The careful study of these drawings will teach us a great deal. It is important to emphasize the difference between a study for a portrait in silverpoint (cat. 29 and 47) or in pen and ink (cat. 46) and a truly representative charcoal portrait (cat. 30 and 41). In his landscape drawings Dürer emerges as a brilliant artist far ahead of his time. Contrast the precise and rigorous forms of a pen and ink drawing, such as *A Forest Spring* (cat. 27), with the conceptual grandeur—combined with precision of detail—of the watercolor sketch, *The Quarry* (cat. 21). All of his talent is equally apparent in the bold landscape, drawn with a brush, *Valley near Kalchreuth* (cat. 22).

In his paintings as in his drawings Dürer strove to place the human figure in space. Since Giotto, Italian art had also been concerned with this problem, through the creation of a space based on perspective. We can thus surmise that Dürer learned this method from a study of the Italian artists. A German art historian has criticized Dürer for his taste for form inspired by Italy and contrasted the young "German" Dürer with the "Italian" Dürer of full maturity. But had Dürer not bridged this decisive turning point between the late Gothic and the Renaissance, German art would probably have stagnated in a medieval provincialism. His example encouraged the spread of Italian art north of the Alps.

While Dürer succeeded in creating volumes and plastic forms by means of line alone, Grünewald gave to his drawings an essentially pictorial quality. In his most important works, like the *Kneeling Figure with Two Angels* (cat. 59), the graphic element plays only a limited role. Grünewald was more concerned with the pictorial values of light and shadow. His preferred medium was chalk, which by tracing heavy lines gives to the drawing its pictorial effect. In many cases the figure is at first only lightly sketched, then accentuated with chalk in the shadowy portions. The work is continued by means of a watercolor *grisaille*, then by highlighting of details, and finally completed by accentuating luminous points with white gouache.

Grünewald is not as expressionistic in his drawings as in his paintings. His originality is most forcefully conveyed in a drawing which depicts the *Head of a Singing Angel* (cat. 61). We would be wrong to consider the exaggerated swelling of the cheek a weakness, as it was intended to accentuate the expressive character of the drawing. If by temperament Grünewald tends toward exaggeration, he is equally capable of translating, in the most delicate manner, emotions of great tenderness and serenity, as he shows for example in his drawing for an Annunciation, *Kneeling Virgin* (cat. 60).

Dürer was never consigned to oblivion by succeeding generations, but Grünewald (whose real name was Mathis Nithart) was only rediscovered at the end of the nineteenth century. A hundred years after his death his name had been forgotten, which is the reason why one of the earliest German art historians, Joachim von Sandrart, mentions him under the incorrect name of Grünewald.

The youthful works of Lucas Cranach the Elder are still more violent in their search for expressive style. The two thieves (cat. 63 and 64), which must have been drawn by Cranach in Vienna shortly after 1500, in the course of a six-year sojourn in that city, would be hard to surpass for sheer horror. Cranach's youthful works were the point of departure for the art of the Danube School, though Cranach himself soon changed his style. Shortly after he moved to Wittenberg, where for the remainder of his life he was to work as official painter to the Elector of Saxony, the spirit of his painting changed, undoubtedly under the influence of Dürer. His style became more serene, moving closer to the Renaissance ideal, as can be seen in his *Lucretia* (cat. 65) and in his *Portrait of a Man* (cat. 67). As for his female figures, they easily explain the adjective graciles by which Melanchthon characterized the art of Cranach. In other works, however, even the most harmonious, Cranach always retained something of the harsh and gnarled style of his youth.

Although no other artist had as great an influence upon the art of his time as did Dürer, the number of his known followers is few. His first pupils were already more or less trained by the time they came to his workshop. Among the most important of these is Hans von Kulmbach. His youthful works, both drawings and engravings, were formerly believed to be works by Dürer himself. Today his style is recognized as being altogether different from that of his teacher. His calm and sentimental nature does not make him any the less original as an artist. One problem in particular relating to the study of Dürer and Kulmbach is raised by a certain monogram of Albrecht Dürer (cat. 24 and 70) found on drawings by both artists. It is probable that all works bearing this particular monogram were once in the collection of Hans Baldung, to whom they had been given. Baldung's collection was purchased by the Strasburg painter Nikolaus Kremer. The latter's widow, sister of the

Strasburg chronicler Sebaldus Büheler, then left the collection to her brother in 1553. In all probability Büheler arbitrarily signed Dürer's monogram to all of the drawings in question. Hence the presence of this monogram in no way attests any relationship to the artist. Each drawing must be carefully studied on stylistic grounds.

Hans Schäufelein, sometimes referred to erroneously in art historical works under the name of Hans Leonhard Schäufeler, worked in Dürer's studio and used the master's models, although he was himself a highly inventive artist. His stocky, rustic figures and the pictorial aspect of his drawings distinguish him sharply from the other artists surrounding Dürer. The brothers Barthel and Sebald Beham, while never pupils of Dürer, reveal his influence in their graphic works. This relationship is more evident in a design by Sebald for a stained glass window (cat. 78) than in drawings by Barthel. The drawings of Peter Flötner (cat. 80 and 81) point to the high quality of creative craftsmanship in the Germany of Dürer's time, that is, before the influence of mannerism loosened the discipline of craftsmanship. Augustin Hirschvogel was the descendant of a family of painters who had come from Bamberg. He served his apprenticeship in Nuremberg, but his drawings reveal only the slightest influence of Dürer. He was less inspired by local artists than by the works of the masters of the Danube School, as can be seen in his *The Castle of Neuburg on the Danube* (cat. 82).

The most important artist of the Dürer circle was Hans Baldung Grien, descended from a family of Swabian humanists. In 1503 he began to frequent Dürer's studio in Nuremberg, where he apparently remained until Dürer's return from Italy. His two altarpieces for the church of Halle-an-der-Saale would thus have been painted in Nuremberg. In 1509 he became an official resident of Strasburg and became master painter there in 1510. He left that city around 1512 for Freiburg, where he painted the altarpiece for the cathedral choir. From 1517 until his death in September 1545 he worked in Strasburg as a painter and designer of woodcuts.

In his drawing *The Beheading of St. Barbara* (cat. 83), probably done before Dürer's departure for Venice, Baldung still seems dependent upon Dürer's example, although the sober and pure linear quality is eminently his own. The same precision, the same freshness are found in his chiaroscuro technique (cat. 85). His predilection for calligraphic line links Baldung to Schongauer, who was Swabian as well and who also emigrated to the Upper Rhine. Of all the draftsmen of Dürer's time, it is Baldung who most clearly reveals the need to express a feeling for beauty, as we can see from his portraits and female figures. No other artist of the period drew as much inspiration from themes of witchcraft. He was prone to combine a formal beauty with the bizarre. Hans Baldung strongly influenced a number of minor masters like Hans Franck (cat. 141) and Hans Leu (cat. 92), who were inspired by his prints. The expression of tumultuous emotions through the dynamism of drawing is a current which even appears in the work of the sculptor H. L. of Breisach, where it assumes, however, excessive proportions.

Heinrich Aldegrever is the only important artist of northwestern Germany (cat. 93) who succeeded, after Dürer, in assimilating the forms of the Renaissance. In this respect he may be compared to the Netherlandish masters. The more serene and gentle temperament of the Swabian artists is altogether distinct from the harsher sensibilities of Franconians like Dürer, Cranach, and Grünewald. Highly productive minor masters like Bernard Strigel, who came from a great family of painters, were able thanks to their origin and sense of balance to make an almost effortless transition between Gothic and Renaissance art. For the most famous artists of this region, the assimilation and interpretation of Italian forms was not as complex a problem as it had been for Dürer.

The center of Swabian art of this period was the imperial city of Augsburg, seat of a vast number of commercial enterprises, the most important of which was that of the Fugger family. The opulence of the city and the open-mindedness of its lords of commerce, whose work with foreign banks brought them into contact with the spirit and forms of the South, made Augsburg the bridgehead of the Renaissance in Germany. The cultural and economic development of Augsburg had begun in the last quarter of the fifteenth century. More artists worked there than anywhere else in Germany. The art of the portrait was well developed in this city, due to the commissions of the ruling class and corporations. According to a note by Matthäus Schwarz, one of Jacob Fugger's treasurers, every rich burgher felt obliged to have his portrait painted at least once. In addition to painted portraits, a large number of portrait drawings have survived, representing every social level of Augsburg from patricians and merchants to the monks of various cloisters, drawn by Hans Holbein the Elder (cat. 96-105) and by other artists of the circle of Master B. B. (cat. 120 and 121).

In the oeuvre of Hans Holbein the Elder portrait drawings occupy the most important place. In fact more than three quarters of his drawings are portraits, but in the majority of cases they were done with a view to establishing a documentary study of facial types, based upon the model books of the Middle Ages. Moreover, certain of these portraits, which are preserved in several small sketchbooks, appear again in altarpieces (cat. 102). Besides these studio records Holbein also made preparatory studies for specific works such as the *Martyrdom of St. Paul* (cat. 95).

If Hans Holbein the Elder was still following the craft traditions of the late Middle Ages, his two sons, Ambrosius and Hans, already belonged to the Renaissance. To the latter their father's art constituted a point of departure. Their own works, moreover, are so closely related that some of them cannot with any degree of certainty be attributed to one brother rather than the other.

The three members of the Holbein family enjoyed a renown which extended far beyond the confines of their native city. One after the other they left Augsburg to settle in Basel. Ambrosius was active there from 1514 to 1519, above all as a portraitist; and it was there that the brilliant Hans Holbein the Younger achieved the full mastery of his art. Deep friendship united the Holbein brothers to Erasmus of Rotterdam, who had also settled in Basel. Hans Holbein the Younger, whose European reputation is based upon his incomparable genius as a portraitist, was also a talented decorator, an aspect of his activity too often neglected. With the exception of a few minor studies almost nothing has survived of his decorative projects. But in his design for the painting of the façade of the *Haus zum Tanz* (cat. 109) his talent as a decorative artist is clearly revealed. The frieze of dancing peasants for this façade is a gem of humor and elegance, breaking with the traditional contemporary concept which portrayed the peasant as a lout.

This project for a mural painting is very different from the later sketch of a decor for a celebration, which represents *Parnassus* (cat. 111). In contrast to the exuberance of the scene for the *Haus zum Tanz* Holbein here uses great economy of means. His drawing of Parnassus quite naturally invites comparison with Raphael's composition on the same subject. The seated figures in the foreground and the grouping of the personages near a bay would lead us to suppose that Holbein was familiar with Raphael's fresco, through the intermediary of an engraving by Marcantonio Raimondi. In this drawing the influence of Mantegna's *Madonna of Victory* is also evident. We can further assume that the rearing horse, from the project for the above mentioned façade, was inspired by the equestrian drawings of Leonardo. It is apparent that Hans Holbein had no difficulty in assimilating the Renaissance, for he seems to resolve, with a natural facility, all the problems which Dürer had been obliged to face. But we must not forget that Holbein was twenty years Dürer's junior, which means that from the very beginnings of his career he was able to profit from the experiments of the Nuremberg Master. Still, his Augsburg origins and the training provided by his father also played a determining role in his artistic evolution.

After the departure of the Holbein dynasty, Hans Burgkmair became the uncontested master of the Augsburg Renaissance. Serving his apprenticeship in his father's studio and later in the workshop of Martin Schongauer, he was, after Dürer, the most productive artist of his age, although he was almost exclusively a woodcut designer. (The Emperor Maximilian, who had always favored Augsburg, gave most of his commissions to Burgkmair, including those of illustrating the Emperor's own writings, such as the *Theuerdank*, the *Weiskunig*, and the *Triumphzug*.) His study here of horses' heads and harnesses (cat. 113) is an example of the great care Burgkmair took with his woodcuts.

Like all the great draftsmen of his time, Burgkmair possessed a mastery of his art that made it possible for him to employ a variety of techniques according to the circumstances or the destination of a drawing. He reveals, however, a definite preference for charcoal or chalk, which is softer still and which best corresponded to his pictorial style. Moreover, it is not unusual for him to add pen and ink to elaborate or highlight the details.

Burgkmair's project for an altarpiece (cat. 112) reveals analogies with the Danube School, and this is still more apparent in his other drawings. It would be an anachronism to speak of a Danube School in the years around 1505 or to speak of its influence upon other regions, but we may conclude, nevertheless, that significant influences of Augsburg origin contributed to the formation of this later school of artists.

The artist most responsible for spreading the artistic tradition of Augsburg is probably Jörg Breu, the most important Augsburg painter after Burgkmair. Breu was active in southern Austria between 1496 and 1502. After establishing himself as a Master in Augsburg the violence of his youthful works softened, and he evolved in the direction of Augsburg painting as represented by Burgkmair (cat. 117 and 118).

The drawings of the monogrammist BB (cat. 120 and 121) raise a special problem. While Winkler considers them, with good reason, to be works by Leonard Beck, to whom he also attributes the *Portrait of Count Moritz von Ertingen* (cat. 79), several reservations have been voiced as to the unity of this group of drawings. It has even been suggested that they represent a souvenir album of Augsburg painters, for which each artist may have contributed his self-portrait. But if we abstract their stylistic similarity this interpretation is hardly viable, since the idea of forming such an album would have been totally alien to the spirit of sixteenth-century artists. More probably, a very early collector assembled a group of drawings of different styles upon which he then affixed this counterfeit monogram. These spurious signatures were undoubtedly intended to pass off the drawings as works by Barthel Beham.

As a pupil of Burgkmair, Wilhelm Ziegler (monogram IZ) may be considered to belong to the group of Swabian-Augsburg artists, the more so as his portrait is included in the collection of portraits by the Master B. B. The monogram IZ found on a number of drawings is part of the coat of arms of the Ziegler family, originally from Creglingen. Thus it is not strictly speaking a monogram but a family seal. The *Portrait of a Young Boy* (cat. 122) by Ziegler is related in its technical execution to Burgkmair, but by its style it is strongly linked to the Danube School. Drawings by Ziegler were also once attributed to an artist of the Danube region, the Master of the Portraits of the Thenn Family. A number of studies attempt to explain Ziegler's works by considering them youthful products of the Messkirch Master (cat. 124), an artist who himself raises many problems. But after 1525 the Messkirch Master emerges as an artist who has reached full maturity. He can be traced until 1550 through an uninterrupted sequence of paintings. Only quite recently has it been suggested that Ziegler's work is attributable to one Peter Strüb the Younger, youngest son of a family of artists living in Veringenstadt (cf. H. D. Ingenhoff, *Der Meister von Sigmaringen, Die Malerfamilie Strüb aus Veringenstadt*, 1962, pp. 45 ff.).

Daniel Hopfer, whose numerous etchings were done for the most part after works by other masters, reveals himself nonetheless in his *Tabernacle for the Holy Sacrament* (cat. 125) worthy of consideration as a draftsman. His technique shows as well a strong debt to Burgkmair.

Around 1500 a new and highly characteristic style developed in the southwestern part of the Empire, in Vienna and lower Austria. Known in the history of German art as the Danube School, it was composed of indigenous Bavarian and Tyrolean elements to which were added Augsburgian and Franconian influences. According to the most recent scholarship, Rueland Frueauf the Younger of Salzburg, the Frankfurter Lucas Cranach the Elder, and the Augsburger Jörg Breu the Elder were the true founders of this school.

The influence of Dürer's graphic art played a considerable role in the development of the new style. The fifteen woodcuts comprising the Apocalypse series, published in 1498, made a strong impression upon the young artists of the time. The "pathetic realism" of Dürer's landscapes was the first element to be adopted by these painters, which they then translated into their own ideal.

In contrast to the Italian artists of the same period, for whom the human figure constituted the unique point of attraction of a painting, the landscape for the masters of the Danube School was no longer simple, rather anonymous decor, but a strongly active element which participated in the dramatic action of the subject. Even within the context of completely localized scenes, the rhythms of nature— birth, death and rebirth—which are also those of human life, monuments, plants, and mountains, were evoked. Alpine landscapes, looming, almost inaccessible, inspired artists who represented them in a highly inventive manner, using lines in the form of curls, or hatching, or lines that were freely strewn over the paper. In a development parallel to the Netherlandish artists, the masters of the Danube School discovered landscape as an autonomous subject. The Netherlandish masters, however, exemplified by Joachim Patenir, tried to represent the diversity of the universe, mountains and rivers, fields and forests, streams and oceans. Conversely, the artists of the southwestern Empire were satisfied with a limited slice of landscape. It was their art, moreover, which influenced the Venetians, and the drawings of Domenico Campagnola, a pupil of Titian, bear the stamp of this influence even in their technique.

In the works of the Danube School human figures and even figures of saints are organically linked to nature. Thus, for example, certain figures take on the gnarled quality of trees, seeming to become one with the landscape. In these works the human form plays a less important role than it did anywhere else in Europe. It should come as no surprise that from this period on there are few figure studies and still fewer portrait drawings in German art.

Another characteristic of the drawings of the Danube School is the predominance of linear elements. In the beginning the tracing is delicate, with the finesse of an engraving, as in the youthful works of Erhard Altdorfer (cat. 133). But this style soon gives way to a larger and freer technique, particularly in the works of Albrecht Altdorfer, brother of Erhard and his artistic superior. This technique constitutes the stylistic signature of the Danube School. In the works of Altdorfer and Wolf Huber line is not merely used to define form and to specify an object, but has, at the same time, its own expressive language.

In spite of the intrinsic value of the graphic elements, these drawings possess real plastic qualities as well. The pictorial effect of these engravings is also due to the tinted background of the paper, which supports the composition of India ink and white gouache. The technique of chiaroscuro upon colored paper, first practiced in Italy, was probably adopted by the masters of the Danube School under the influence of Dürer and his disciples.

Albrecht and Erhard Altdorfer were the sons of the painter Ulrich of Regensburg, none of whose works survive. By 1505 both Albrecht and Erhard knew of the Danube School. Albrecht was probably influenced by Jörg Kölderer, official court painter to the Emperor Maximilian, who was active in Innsbruck, as well as by Lucas Cranach. (One proof of the ties which linked Cranach to the artists of the Danube School is provided by the drawing representing a *Landscape with Lovers* (cat. 126) and by woodcuts executed for the cloister of Mondsee im Salzkammergut.) It was only after settling in Regensburg that Albrecht Altdorfer's true artistic personality developed. His intensive artistic activity is demonstrated as much by his easel paintings as by his murals and engravings. He was an architect as well and a member of the municipal council of his native city. Among the numerous artists who drew their inspiration from Albrecht Altdorfer's style, we must first mention the painter's own brother, although the latter remained in Albrecht's company for only a relatively short period. By 1510-11 he was working in southern Austria, and from 1512 until his death he was official painter to the court of the Princes of Mecklenburg.

The works of the *Master of the Historia Friderici et Maximiliani* are linked stylistically to those of Albrecht Altdorfer that predate 1510, but there is no evidence of a master-disciple relationship. The suggestion has been made recently that the Master of the Historia was Niklaus Breu, the younger brother of Jörg Breu the Elder.

Wolf Huber was the youngest artist of the Danube School and his art is scarcely less important than that of Albrecht Altdorfer. Born in Feldkirch, he was for many years painter to the Bishops of Passau. The evolution of his art is reflected, more than in Altdorfer, in his drawings. There is a definite continuity between the *Landscape with a Fortress* (cat. 135), with its delicate strokes, the drawings with or without wash (cat. 137), and the *View of the City* (cat. 140), with its pronounced pictorial quality. Although Huber drew with pen on untinted paper his drawings already possess a pictorial character. Further, his talent as a painter is revealed in the watercolor *Lower Alpine Landscape* (cat. 137). Huber was also the only artist of the Danube School whose studies of heads are almost finished portraits (cat. 138). The majority of his drawings are executed on brick-red paper.

Like all the masters of the Danube School, the Swiss artists made spontaneous and expressive line the dominant element of the drawing. The representation of landscape, however, plays a relatively modest role in the work of the Swiss masters, as opposed to the artists of southwestern Germany. Actual landscapes such as we find in Altdorfer's work or specific views as in Huber are exceptions here. Tradition has it, nevertheless, that Hans Leu made drawings of the landscape around Mount Gisli a few weeks before his death. But whatever the truth of this, Swiss artists in general were more concerned with the human figure.

The most talented Swiss artist of the sixteenth century was Urs Graf, a native of Solothurn. His bellicose temperament led him to volunteer as a mercenary, which was the source of many of his adventures; and in peacetime fits of temper and a maladjusted life were the cause of many altercations with the law. The subjects of a great number of his drawings—pen and ink for the most part—were taken from the life of mercenaries and camp followers. His violent nature is reflected in his turbulent style, but gifted artist that he was, he was also capable of a calm and harmonious line, as the drawings shown here will reveal.

27

Niklaus Manuel Deutsch was the son of Emmanuel Alleman, a pharmacist born near Turin who married a woman from Bern. His son took his father's first name as part of his own and translated "Alleman" into "Deutsch." During one part of his life he wrote poetry and religious plays. After 1521 he was almost exclusively involved with diplomatic and political missions for his native city, traveling with the Swiss army to Italy in the capacity of military historian without officially being a soldier. Like Urs Graf he took the "Swiss dagger" as an element of his signature, as we can see from his numerous drawings. Niklaus Manuel's taste for elegance of form, far more pronounced than in the work of other Swiss artists, can undoubtedly be explained by his Italian descent. Even in his first drawings he reveals himself to be far more refined and harmonious than the turbulent Urs Graf. That he was well acquainted with the Italian art of the Renaissance is clearly seen in the drawings of his maturity, as for example *The Virgin with the Infant Christ* (cat. 150). His artistic career ended at just that moment when his talent achieved its greatest height.

Like Hans Leu of Zurich, Deutsch complained that from the second decade of the century his art had no longer permitted him to earn his livelihood. Ulrich Zwingli and the other Swiss leaders of the Reformation took the Old Testament's injunction against the worship of images and made it an important element of their own doctrine. Not only did they remove paintings and sculpture from the churches but they were equally opposed to their replacement by other works of art. Artists were deprived of their principal source of income, the production of altarpieces. It was to be a long time before Swiss painting recovered from this blow.

Hans Leu was a lyrical painter who was highly receptive to outside influences. Around the year 1510 he is believed to have visited Dürer. After his return to Zurich in 1515 he moved closer toward the art of Baldung Grien and Hans Holbein, whose work had an influence upon his style of drawing. But his landscapes, conversely, bring Leu closer to the masters of the Danube School. Two studies of trees (Dessau, Nuremberg) are still attributed both to Hans Leu and Erhard Altdorfer.

In attempting to characterize the whole of German drawing at the time of Dürer, we note that the search for expressiveness and concern with harmony seem to constitute its two dominant artistic tendencies. Each artist, according to his own sensibility and local tradition, leans toward one or the other of these poles. The artists of Augsburg drew closer to the classical ideal of the Renaissance, while the masters of the Danube School, at least in their early works, show a greater reserve in the face of the new artistic spirit. But the evolution of an artist such as Albrecht Altdorfer reveals, nonetheless, a growing purity of form in the spirit of the Renaissance. The essential contribution of the Danube School, however, remains the discovery of landscape.

All artistic inspiration of this period, though, turned to the genius of Dürer as its point of departure and reached its culmination in this artist's work. From his earliest drawings Dürer effected the decisive transition from late Gothic realism and the Netherlandish tradition to the humanism of the Renaissance. He is the only German artist to embody all the aspirations of his time and who, beyond the boundaries of his own country, served as an example to his contemporaries and to future generations.

Dr. Fedja Anzelewski

Abbreviations

1. *Frequently mentioned publications*

Altdorfer-Exhibition	Albrecht Altdorfer und sein Kreis, memorial exhibition for the 400th anniversary of Altdorfer's death. Official catalogue, Munich, 1938.
Baldung-Grien	Hans Baldung Grien, exhibition at the Staatliche Kunsthalle Karlsruhe, under the patronage of ICOM, second revised edition, 1959.
Buchner-Feuchtmayr	E. Buchner-K. Feuchtmayr: Beiträge zur Geschichte der deutschen Kunst. 2 vols., 1924-28.
Deutsche Zeichnungen 1400-1900	Catalogue of the traveling exhibition, Deutsche Zeichnungen 1400-1900, Introduction by Peter Halm, 1956.
Die Malerfamilie Holbein	Die Malerfamilie Holbein in Basel, exhibition at the Kunstmuseum, Basel, during the 500th anniversary of the University of Basel, 1960.
Friedländer-Bock	Staatliche Museen zu Berlin. Die Zeichnungen alter Meister im Kupferstichkabinett, published by Max J. Friedländer. Die deutschen Meister, detailed catalogue by Elfried Bock, 2 vols., 1921.
Friedländer-Bock Handzeichnungen	Max J. Friedländer and Elfried Bock: Handzeichnungen deutscher Meister des 15. und 16. Jahrhunderts.
Ganz Handzeichnungen	P. Ganz: Handzeichnungen schweizerischer Meister des 15. bis 18. Jahrhunderts (ca. 1904-07).
Lippmann-Grote	Zeichnungen alter Meister im Kupferstichkabinett der Kgl. Museen zu Berlin. Herausgegeben von der Direktion. 2 vols., 1910.

Lugt	Frits Lugt: Les Marques de Collections de Dessins et d'Estampes, 2 vols., 1921-56.
Meister um Albrecht Dürer	Meister um Albrecht Dürer, exhibition at the Germanisches National-Museum, Nuremberg, 1961. (Anzeiger des Germanischen National-Museums 1960-61.)
Schönbrunner-Meder	Handzeichnungen alter Meister aus der Albertina und anderen Sammlungen. Published by Joseph Schönbrunner and Joseph Meder. 12 vols., 1896-1908.
Springer Federzeichnungen	J. Springer: 20 Federzeichnungen altdeutscher Meister aus dem Besitz des königl. Kupferstichkabinetts zu Berlin.
Thieme-Becker	H. Thieme und U. Becker: Allgemeines Lexikon der bildenden Künstler, 37 vols., 1907-50.
Winkler Altdeutsche Zeichnungen	Friedrich Winkler: Altdeutsche Zeichnungen (Zeichnungen des Kupferstichkabinetts Berlin), 1947.
Winkler Slg. Ehlers	F. Winkler: Altdeutsche Meisterzeichnungen aus der Sammlung Ehlers im Berliner Kupferstichkabinett, 1939.
Voss Donaustil	Hermann Voss: Der Ursprung des Donaustils, 1907.

2. *Periodicals*

ASAK	Anzeiger für Schweizerische Altertumskunde
BM	Berliner Museen
GK	Die graphischen Künste
JKSAK	Jahrbuch der kunsthistorischen Sammlungen der allerhöchsten Kaiserhauses, Wien
JKSW	Jahrbuch der kunsthistorischen Sammlungen in Wien
JKW	Jahrbücher für Kunstwissenschaft
JPKS	Jahrbuch der (königlich) preussischen Kunstsammlungen
MJBK	Münchner Jahrbuch für bildende Kunst
MJKW	Marburger Jahrbuch für Kunstwissenschaft
MKW	Monatshefte für Kunstwissenschaft
OMD	Old Master Drawings
ORK	Oberrheinische Kunst. Jahrbuch der oberrheinischen Museen
P	Pantheon
RKW	Repertorium für Kunstwissenschaft

ST-J	Städel-Jahrbuch
WJKG	Wiener Jahrbuch für Kunstgeschichte
WRJ	Wallraf-Richartz-Jahrbuch
ZBK	Zeitschrift für bildende Kunst
ZCHK	Zeitschrift für christliche Kunst
ZDVKW	Zeitschrift des deutschen Vereins für Kunstwissenschaft
ZHWKK	Zeitschrift für historische Waffen- und Kostümkunde
ZKG	Zeitschrift für Kunstgeschichte
ZKW	Zeitschrift für Kunstwissenschaft (= Zeitschrift des Deutschen Vereins für Kunstwissenschaft, Neue Folge)

3. *Other Abbreviations*

Diss.	Dissertation
KdZ	Catalogue of drawings in the Berlin Print Room

The dimensions are given in millimeters and inches, height preceding width.

Catalogue

MARTIN SCHONGAUER

Painter and engraver. Born around 1453 in Colmar. Son of the goldsmith Caspar Schongauer, a native of Augsburg. Died on February 2, 1491, in Breisach, where he had completed the fresco of the *Last Judgment*.

BIBLIOGRAPHY: J. Rosenberg, *Schongauers Handzeichnungen* (Diss. Munich), 1923; Id., *Martin Schongauers Handzeichnungen*, 1923; E. Flechsig, *Martin Schongauer*, 1951; F. Winzinger, *Die Zeichnungen Martin Schongauers*, 1962.

1. *St. Dorothy, Seated*

Pen and gray-brown ink. 176 x 165 mm, 7 x 6½ in. KdZ 1015.

BIBLIOGRAPHY: Friedländer-Bock, p. 77; Rosenberg, p. 90; Id., *Handzeichnungen*, p. 36, no. 48; Flechsig, p. 385; Winzinger, no. 37.

The drawing as a whole reveals Schongauer's drawing technique with exceptional clarity. He first lightly sketched the composition; this is especially noticeable in the drawing of the Child, for in the finished drawing the artist has moved away considerably from the preliminary sketch. After the preparatory study he super-imposed lines in the course of different working periods and heightened the work with strong accents of dark brown ink, as in the garment on the left. Rosenberg was dubious about the authenticity of this drawing. However, the draftsmanship points strongly to a Schongauer attribution. Winzinger speaks of it as "a mature and classical work" related to the artist's late engravings such as *Arms with Unicorn* (B.97).

2. *Bust of an Old Man Wearing Fur Collar and Fur Hat*

Pen and brown ink. 104 x 71 mm, 4⅛ x 2¾ in. The two upper corners, mono-gram, and frame added later by another hand.

Coll. Didot (Lugt 119) and Heseltine (Lugt 1507). Acquired 1913. KdZ 4917.

BIBLIOGRAPHY: Catalogue of the coll. Firmin-Didot, 1877, no. 41; *Original Draw-ings Chiefly of the German School in the Collection of J.P.H.* (Heseltine), 1912, no. 31; M. Lehrs, in *Mitt. aus den sächs. Kunstslgn.* 5, 1914, pp. 6 ff.; Friedländer-Bock, p. 77; Rosenberg, Diss., p. 74; Id., *Handzeichnungen*, p. 24; K. Bauch, in *ORK* 5, 1932, p. 183; Winkler, *Altdeutsche Zeichnungen*, p. 9; J. Baum, *Martin Schongauer*, 1948, p. 45; Flechsig, p. 325; F. Winzinger, *Deutsche Meisterzeich-nungen der Gotik*, 1949, p. 48; Id. in *Die Kunst*, 1950/51, p. 46; K. Bauch, "Bild-nisse Martin Schongauers," in *Studien zur Kunst des Oberrheins, Festschrift für Werner Noack*, 1958, pp. 78, 80; Winzinger, no. 27.

The concept of this head of an elderly man is more closely related to that of a portrait than are the other studies of heads by Schongauer. This highly individual concept, with its almost frontal portrayal and lively expression, caused Lehrs to consider it a self-portrait. Only the relatively early date of its creation, toward the mid seventies, contradicts this thesis. This page, as well as the drawings *Head of a Spy* (Winzinger 10) and *Monk Holding a Pitcher* (Winzinger 13), is considered to be the closest to an authentic portrait among the works of the master. There is also a certain similarity in physiognomy between this head and that of the apostle Philip in the engraving of that name (B.38).

SCHOOL OF MARTIN SCHONGAUER

3. *St. Margaret*

Pen and brown and black ink. 217 x 131 mm, 8½ x 5⅛ in. Upper corners rounded.

Coll. v. Nagler (Lugt 2529). Acquired 1835. KdZ 1016.

4. *St. Dorothy*

Pen and black ink. 214 x 122 mm, 8½ x 4¾ in. Upper corners rounded.

Coll. v. Nagler (Lugt 2529). Acquired 1835. KdZ 1017.

BIBLIOGRAPHY: M. Lehrs in *Mitt. aus den sächs. Kunstslgn.* 5, 1914, no. 6; Friedländer-Bock, p. 77; Rosenberg, Diss. p. 96; Id., *Handzeichnungen*, p. 34; M. Lehrs in *The Burlington Magazine*, 1924, p. 134; Winzinger, nos. 82/83.

These pages, always considered as an ensemble in the literature, are among the best drawings in the circle of the master. It is not surprising then that for a while Rosenberg considered them to be works by Schongauer. The two drawings are related to the engraving *St. Agnes* (B.62) and show to what extent the artist attempted to imitate, even to the line, Schongauer's model. The imitator's hand is more easily distinguished in the drawing of *St. Dorothy* than in this drawing of *St. Margaret*. There the expression on the saint's face is rather weak and vacant. But the *St. Margaret* could well be an authentic Schongauer. Winzinger justly considers the delicate preliminary sketch, which is still perceptible, to be characteristic of the drawings by the master himself.

NUREMBERG MASTER, ca. 1480

5. *Half-Length Study of a Woman*

Pen and brown ink. 134 x 103 mm, 5¼ x 4⅛ in.

Coll. Koller and v. Lanna. Acquired 1910. KdZ 4464.

BIBLIOGRAPHY: Schönbrunner-Meder, no. 1284; Friedländer-Bock, p. 89.

In this drawing, as in the *Baptism of Christ* (cat. 6), there are obvious Schongauer influences. We find, however, in the woman's expression much of the harshness seen in portraits by Michael Wolgemut, as may be proved by a comparison with the latter's *Portrait of Ursula Hans Tucher* (1478) in the Museum in Kassel (cf. E. Buchner: *Das deutsche Bildnis der Spätgotik und der frühen Dürerzeit*, 1953, pl. 140). There would thus be grounds for considering Dürer's master to be the author of this impressive drawing.

NUREMBERG MASTER

6. *The Baptism of Christ*

Pen and brown ink. 138 x 117 mm, 5⅞ x 4⅝ in. Watermark: part of the head of an ox with suspended orb.

Coll. Grahl. Acquired 1912. KdZ 4619.

BIBLIOGRAPHY: E. Abraham, *Nürnberger Malerei in der zweiten Hälfte des 15. Jahrhunderts*, 1912, p. 211; Friedländer-Bock, p. 89.

The presentation of this composition within a medallion leads us to conclude that it was probably a design for a window. The strong influence of the art of the Middle and Upper Rhine is evident. The arms of the Fürleger family at the bottom of the drawing indicate that the unknown draftsman worked in Nuremberg.

THE HOUSEBOOK MASTER—ERHARD REUWICH

Painter, miniaturist, engraver, designer of woodcuts, glass-painter, and publisher. Active between 1475 and 1500 in the region of the central Rhine, probably in Mainz.

BIBLIOGRAPHY: H. Th. Bossert-W. F. Storck, *Das Mittelalterliche Hausbuch*. After the original book in the possession of the prince of Waldburg-Wolfegg-Waldsee, commissioned by the Deutscher Verein für Kunstwissenschaft; F. Winkler, *Mittel-niederrheinische und westfälische Handzeichnungen des 15. und 16. Jahrhunderts* (*Die Meisterzeichnung* 4), 1932; J. Dürkop in *ORK* 5, 1932, pp. 83 ff.; Count E. of Solms-Laubach in *St J* 9, 1935-36, pp. 13 ff.; J. C. J. Bierens de Haan, *De Meester van het Amsterdamsche Kabinett*, 1947; Count J. Waldburg-Wolfegg, *Das Mittelalterliche Hausbuch, Betrachtungen vor einer Bilderhandschrift*, 1957; A. Stange, *Der Hausbuchmeister* (*Studien zur Deutschen Kunstgeschichte* 316), 1958.

7. *A Prince at Table*

Pen and brown ink. 277 x 192 mm, 11 x 7½ in.

Coll. v. Lanna (Lugt 2773). Acquired 1910. KdZ 4442.

BIBLIOGRAPHY: A. Warburg-M. J. Friedländer in *JPKS* 32, 1911, pp. 180 ff.; Bossert-Storck, p. 46; H. Leonhard-H. Th. Bossert in *ZBK* 1912, p. 242, note 2; Friedländer-Bock, p. 71; Winkler, no. 13; Dürkop, p. 134; Count of Solms-Laubach, pp. 36, 62; Count Waldburg-Wolfegg, p. 35; Stange, no. 108.

Friedländer was the first to attribute this drawing incontrovertibly to the Housebook Master, and his attribution has never been seriously questioned. The artist has deftly sketched the scene with rapid, light strokes of the pen. Only the figure of the prince seated alone under a baldaquin, that of the servant standing in front of the table, and the head of the man to the left of the prince have been executed in detail. A. Warburg rightly considered this scene to represent the Emperor Maximilian at the Banquet of the Peace of Bruges in the year 1488. Maximilian, who was imprisoned by the City of Bruges from May 5 to 16 of 1488, can be identified as a German by his headdress, which distinguishes him from the other figures mainly wearing hats. The prince is also the only one still wearing long pointed shoes in the late Gothic style; the other personages wear the wide shoes already popular in the Netherlands at this time. The principal figure, who is drawn again on the verso of this sheet, is still more easily identifiable as Maximilian. There the prince is portrayed kneeling and praying at Mass. This scene of the Banquet of the Peace shows in its composition a close similarity to the illustration of the January page by the Limbourg brothers in the *Très Riches Heures* of the Duke Jean de Berry (ca. 1415). That page represents the prince seated at the table with a monk. There, as in the Berlin drawing, courtiers and onlookers crowd around the table, in front of which stands a servant carrying a cloth on his shoulder. The same composition reappears in the Grimmani Breviary (ca. 1510).

Solms-Laubach has called attention to a Flemish miniature (Solms-Laubach, pl. 45) in the Bibliothèque Royale in Brussels which prefigures the drawing on the verso of our sheet. Thus it is legitimate to presume the miniature influenced the Housebook Master, all the more so as Erhard Reuwich left us several examples of his own work as a manuscript illuminator.

8. *Three Men in Conversation*

Pen and brown ink. 162 x 104 mm, 6⅜ x 4⅛ in.

Coll. Rodrigues (Lugt 897). Acquired 1904. KdZ 4291.

BIBLIOGRAPHY: J. Springer in *JPKS* 26, 1905, p. 68; Id., *Federzeichnungen*, pl. 2; W. F. Storck in *MKW* 2, 1909, p. 262, no. 6; L. Baer in *MKW* 3, 1910, p. 408; Lippmann-Grote, 2nd ed., no. 137; Bossert-Storck, p. 45; Friedländer-Bock, p. 71; Winkler, no. 11; Dürkop, p. 114; Count of Solms-Laubach, p. 90; Winkler, *Altdeutsche Zeichnungen*, p. 9; Bierens de Haan, *Deutsche Zeichnungen 1400-1900*, no. 16; Count Waldburg-Wolfegg, p. 12; Stange, no. 109.

Although this sheet was drawn with more care than the preceding one, the artist's hand is easily recognizable in the disposition of the heads, the rendering of the hair, and the typical treatment of the hands. Its former title, *The Paternal Warning*, does not seem appropriate. More probably it depicts a conversation, as in the etching *Two Hunters with a Dog* (Stange 71). The costumes as well as the rather timorous quality of the draftsmanship would seem to indicate an earlier execution. This genre scene may be dated around 1480 as it still clearly recalls the drawings of the Housebook.

MASTER OF THE STÖTTERITZ ALTAR

Nuremberg painter active around 1480.

9. *Study for a Triptych*

Pen and brown ink. 210 x 315 mm, 8¼ x 12½ in. Upper left corner torn off.

Coll. of King Friedrich-Wilhelm I. KdZ 1031.

BIBLIOGRAPHY: Lippmann-Grote, 2nd ed., no. 138; Friedländer-Bock, p. 78; F. Winkler in *JPKS* 60, 1939, pp. 212 ff.

The anonymous draftsman established the tripartite composition in a grandly conceived sketch. On the left, Christ praying on the Mount of Olives; center, the Crucifixion; on the right, the Resurrection. The lettering on the garments indicates the colors which the artist intended to give them. This drawing, formerly considered to be a work by Schongauer, has been identified by Winkler as a project for the altarpiece of the church of Stötteritz, near Dresden. The composition of the three panels was further elaborated in the course of their execution. The artist, nonetheless, held exactly to his original plan where the colors were concerned. The style of the painting points to a master who was probably active in Nuremberg around 1480 and a follower of Hans Pleydenwurff (d. 1472). This is the only original study for an altarpiece of the fifteenth century in the Berlin Museum. The altarpiece existed until World War II, but its fate since then is unknown.

MICHAEL WOLGEMUT

Painter and designer of woodcuts. Born in Nuremberg in 1434. After spending some time in Munich he inherited the Nuremberg studio of Hans Pleydenwurff after the latter's death in 1472. He died in Nuremberg in 1519.

10. *Group of Five Standing Men*

Pen and black-brown ink, on red tinted paper. 257 x 187 mm, 10⅛ x 7⅜ in.

Coll. v. Nagler (Lugt 2529). Acquired 1835. KdZ 1027.

BIBLIOGRAPHY: Springer, *Federzeichnung*, pl. 3; Friedländer-Bock, p. 89; F. J. Stadler, *Michael Wolgemut und der Nürnberger Holzschnitt im letzten Drittel des 15. Jahrhunderts*, 1913, p. 86.

The Berlin catalogue attributes this drawing to Dürer's teacher, with reservations. It probably represents a group at the foot of the Cross. Stadler calls attention to the relationships between this drawing and a group of drawings on reddish paper (Library of the University of Erlangen) that were not executed by Wolgemut but which come from the circle around his workshop. Nevertheless, the Berlin drawing may be considered to be by the master, thanks to studies in progress on Wolgemut's work, particularly those concerned with the separation of his work from that of his stepson, Wilhelm Pleydenwurff (1458-1494). See R. Bellm: *Wolgemuts Skizzenbuch im Berliner Kupferstichkabinett. Ein Beitrag zur Erforschung des graphischen Werkes von Michael Wolgemut und Wilhelm Pleydenwurff, Studien z. deut. Kunstgesch.*, no. 332, 1959; and G. Betz, *Der Nürnberger Maler Michael Wolgemut (1434-1519) und seine Werkstatt. Ein Beitrag zur Geschichte der spätgotischen Malerei in Franken.* Diss. Freiburg, 1955.

VEIT STOSS

Sculptor, painter, and engraver. Born in 1447/48 in Dinkelsbühl. Renounced his Augsburg citizenship in 1477 and left for Cracow. Returned to Nuremberg in 1496 and remained there until his death in 1533, in spite of the severe punishment inflicted upon him by the Council of Nuremberg for the crime of fraud.

11. *Presentation at the Temple*

Pen and brown ink. Watermark: small circle. 114 x 178 mm, 4½ x 7 in. Inscribed on the verso, in the artist's hand: "feyt stuos 1505" with the master's mark.

Coll. Campe (Lugt 1391) and Ehlers. Acquired 1939. KdZ 17 653.

BIBLIOGRAPHY: E. Baumeister in *MJBK*, n.s. 4, 1927, p. 386; E. Schilling, *Nürnberger Handzeichnungen des 15. und 16. Jahrhunderts (Die Meisterzeichnung 3)*, 1929, no. 8; Winkler, *Slg Ehlers* no. 3; Id. in *JPKS* 60, 1939, no. 13; E. Lutze, *Veit Stoss*, 1952, p. 41.

The Berlin drawing is the only one by this renowned sculptor which was conceived as a finished work. His other drawings are a large working sketch in Cracow for the Bamberg altarpiece and two sketches on a draft of a letter, now in Budapest. The *Presentation at the Temple* shares many characteristics with engravings by the same artist.

Stoss created this page during one of the most tragic periods of his life; nearly sixty, he went bankrupt after being publicly disgraced and forced to pay damages.

WOLFGANG KATZHEIMER

Painter, designer of windows and woodcuts. Mentioned in Bamberg from 1478 to 1508.

BIBLIOGRAPHY: F. Winkler in *B M* 56, 1935, p. 79; M. Müller and F. Winkler in *JPKS* 58, 1937, pp. 241 ff.; H. Muth, *Aigentliche Abbildung der Statt Bamberg,*

Ansichten von Bamberg aus vier Jahrhunderten, 1957; Id., *Die Ansichten der Stadt Bamberg vom Ausgang des 15. Jahrhunderts bis zur Mitte des 19. Jahrhunderts, Eine Studie zur Entwicklungsgeschichte der Stadtvedute* (Diss. Würzburg, 1953-54), 96; *Bericht des Historischen Vereins Bamberg*, 1958.

12. *The Imperial and Episcopal Palace on the Domberg in Bamberg*

Pen and brown ink, with gouache and watercolor. Watermark: head of an ox. 190 x 472 mm, 7 ½ x 18 ⅝ in. Acquired 1935. KdZ 15 346.

BIBLIOGRAPHY: Müller-Winkler, p. 241, no. 1.

The former imperial palace was located adjacent to the north end of the cathedral, on the present site of the "Old Court." At the left of the drawing is a polygonal chapel of the Romanesque period with a Gothic choir. A gabled dwelling is linked to the chapel by a low corridor. A large thirteenth-century hall adjoins the living quarters. This group of buildings, separated from the entrance to the cathedral square by a crenellated wall and gateway, is terminated at the right by a fortified wooden gallery.

We find the same group of buildings in a drawing in the British Museum (reproduced by C. Dodgson in *Old Master Drawings*, vol. 1, 1926-27, pl. 30) that depicts the trial by fire of the Empress Kunigunde. The same scene is also reproduced in a painting, now in a private collection in Munich, that shows the former imperial palace in the background. The paintings and the London drawing differ principally in the construction of the upper part of the tower: instead of the wooden gallery they show a timber superstructure with four slender corner turrets. The transformation of the upper story of the tower is mentioned in 1489. The new construction was probably necessitated by a fire that took place in 1487. Thus the Berlin drawing undoubtedly shows the appearance of the site before that date.

Like the London drawing, the painting (executed between 1489, the year of reconstruction, and 1509, the date of the woodcut by Wolf Trauts based on the painting) is accepted as a work by Wolfgang Katzheimer. The latter was the only well-known Bamberg artist of the end of the fifteenth century. There is a close relationship in technical execution between the Berlin and London drawings that makes the Katzheimer attribution of the drawing shown here well-founded, despite the differences in date of the two pages.

13. *The "Court of the Burgraves" on the Domberg in Bamberg*

Pen and black ink, with watercolor and gouache. Watermark: head of an ox. 237 x 392 mm, 9 ⅜ x 15 ½ in. Acquired 1935. KdZ 15 343.

BIBLIOGRAPHY: Müller-Winkler, no. 7; Muth, *Aigentliche Abbildung*, pl. 4; Winkler, *Altdeutsche Zeichnungen*, p. 13.

This group of buildings shows one of the most important religious structures in Bamberg, seen from the moat of the old city. The watchtower on the left is the old Tower of Jacob or *porta occidentalis* of the ancient Babenberg Castle. The tower also serves as a gate, as may be seen from the lowered portcullis. The characteristic roof of the tower reappears in a painting of *Christ Bearing the Cross* (see cat. 14), where the background also shows the city of Bamberg. This painting is in the Church of St. Sebaldus, Nuremberg. Thanks to the position of the tower the exact site of the building can be determined. This drawing cannot predate 1500.

14. Above: *The Curia Buildings of the Cathedral, on the Grounds of the New Episcopal Residence in Bamberg*

Below: *The Cloister of Michelsberg in Bamberg*

Pen and brown ink, with watercolor and gouache. Watermark: Gothic "p" (Briquet no. 8689). 275 x 349 mm, 10⅞ x 13¾ in. Acquired 1935. KdZ 15 344.

BIBLIOGRAPHY: Müller-Winkler, nos. 4 and 5.

In another drawing in the Berlin Print Room (KdZ 15 342) we find the same group of curia buildings, seen from the same point, but somewhat more detailed in execution and extended farther toward the right. In the London drawing that shows the site at a later date, these same buildings are situated to the right of the tower, separated by a small street. The curia buildings occupied the site where the new Residence stands today.

We find once again in *Christ Bearing the Cross* of 1485 commissioned by Hans Tucher the Elder (St. Sebaldus, Nuremberg, Muth, pl. 2), the view of the cloister of Michelsberg, above the City of Bamberg, rendered faithfully to the last detail. This drawing was probably executed before 1485. The view of the cloister is seen from the rose garden of the present Residence. On the verso (not illustrated) is the Church of the Carmelites seen from the Domberg.

MASTER OF THE DRAPERY STUDIES

Active in the upper Rhine region between 1470 and 1500.

15. Recto: *Studies for an Entombment or a Lamentation*

Pen and black ink, with partial wash. Watermark: Gothic "p" with a flower (Briquet no. 8608). 275 x 195 mm, 10⅞ x 7⅝ in.

Coll: Lawrence (Lugt 2445) and Hausmann (Lugt 378). Acquired 1875. KdZ 2628.

BIBLIOGRAPHY: Friedländer-Bock, p. 92; E. Buchner in *MJBK* 4, 1927, pp. 288 ff.; F. Winkler in *WRJ*, n.s. 1, 1930, pp. 123 ff.

A series of drawings at Coburg Castle was formerly attributed to the circle around the Housebook Master. E. Buchner added to these another group of drawings which he attributed to an independent artist. Because of the unusual round shape of the Coburg drawings, the artist received the name of the Master of the Coburg Roundels. Since in the ever-growing number of drawings attributed to this master drapery studies occupy a large place, he is today referred to as the Master of the Drapery Studies. A large number of these drawings are copies based on works by other artists.

The drawing pictured here reveals the particular nature of these studies of drapery. The outline is always done in pen and ink, then completed in wash, sometimes with additions of white highlights. Here the wash is only applied to the bottom of the garment worn by the weeping Magdalen, who is copied from a Schongauer engraving, *The Entombment* (B.18). The verso of the drawing (not illustrated) shows a seated figure above, probably God the Father, or the Christ of a Coronation of the Virgin. It is impossible to define clearly the iconographic context of the two kneeling figures.

MONOGRAMMIST MFP OF 1495

16. *Five Pairs of Fencers*

Pen and black ink. 311 x 413 mm, 12¼ x 16¼ in. The letters MFP inscribed on upper edge, dated below 1495.

Original collection. KdZ 2674.

BIBLIOGRAPHY: Friedländer-Bock, p. 70; J. B. Shaw in *OMD* 10, 1935/36, pl. 66; Winkler in *ZKW* 3, 1949, p. 68.

Until now this page has not been very highly esteemed in the literature, although the studies of movements as well as those of the heads reveal fine qualities of observation in this draftsman. Shaw has found points of comparison between this sheet and a drawing in Rennes signed MF and dated 1499, whose subject is a seated female saint. The Rennes drawing, however, shows a much greater Schongauer influence than does the one in Berlin. Winkler considers that there is a connection, although "not well defined as yet," between these two sheets and a drawing in Copenhagen that portrays the Holy Family. He attributes the Copenhagen drawing to the illustrator of the *Buch der Beispiele der Alten Weisen* (Bidpai), published in Urach by Konrad Fyner around 1481. The Berlin group of fencers seems closer to the "Bidpai" master from Urach than does the Rennes drawing.

From a thematic point of view this page is closely related to the treatises on fencing which were published in the fifteenth century. Nevertheless, it has nothing in common with the different manuscripts of the treatise on fencing said to be by Talhoff, published in the second half of the century in the region of Lake Constance and the Upper Rhine. Although the different thrusts and stances of fencing are well observed and faithfully reproduced, it is unlikely that this drawing was destined for a book on fencing. The repeated composition of two groups of fencers seen in perspective rather suggests a decorative purpose, perhaps a design for a table top, following the example of Hans Holbein the Younger (Eidgenössisches Landesmuseum, Zurich).

ALBRECHT DÜRER

Painter, engraver, etcher, designer of woodcuts and windows, theoretician of art. Born May 25, 1471, in Nuremberg. Traveled during 1490-94. First trip to Venice after his marriage in 1494, where he remained until the beginning of 1495. Second Venetian sojourn during 1505-07. Worked for the Emperor Maximilian from 1512 to 1519. Netherlands trip in 1520-21. Died in Nuremberg on June 4, 1528.

BIBLIOGRAPHY: *Zeichnungen von Albrecht Dürer in Nachbildungen*, ed. by F. Lippmann, 7 vols. (vols. 6 and 7 published by F. Winkler), 1883-1929; H. Tietze, E. Tietze, and Conrat, *Kritisches Verzeichnis der Werke Albrecht Dürers*, 2 parts in 3 vols., 1928-1938; E. Flechsig, *Albrecht Dürer, Sein Leben und seine künstlerische Entwicklung*, 2 vols., 1928-31; F. Winkler, *Die Zeichnungen Albrecht Dürers*, 4 vols., 1936-1939; E. Panofsky, *The Life and Art of Albrecht Dürer*, 2 vols., 1st ed. 1945; F. Winkler, *Albrecht Dürer, Leben und Werk*, 1957. It is impossible to list here all the works dealing with Dürer's drawings, for the bibliography is too vast. The older works are listed in the books by Friedländer-Bock, Winkler, *Dürer-Zeichnungen*, Tietze, and Panofsky.

17. *Virgin Enthroned with the Infant Christ and Two Angel Musicians*

Pen and brown ink. The flesh is heightened with pale reddish watercolor. 210 x

147 mm, 8¼ x 5¾ in. Signed "d" below the line of the frame and dated 1485. Subsequently inscribed A.d.

Coll. Posonyi-Hulot. Acquired 1877. KdZ 1.

BIBLIOGRAPHY: Lippmann, no. 1; Friedländer-Bock, p. 21; Tietze, no. 2; Flechsig, II, p. 265; Winkler, *Zeichnungen*, no. 4; Panofsky, no. 649; Winkler, *Dürer*, pp. 2, 9.

Dürer made this drawing, with its highly finished execution, at the age of 14. It seems to be a completely original work, indebted neither to Wolgemut nor Schongauer. The even line of this drawing can, at most, be linked with studies of Schongauer's etchings. Any model, if one is to be found, must undoubtedly be sought in Netherlandish art. The preceding owner is said to have had in his possession a model that was probably of the same type as the *Virgin in a Niche* by the Master of Flémalle. Panofsky thinks the model for the Dürer drawing was more likely of Nuremberg origin.

18. *Three Lansquenets*

Pen and blackish-brown ink. 220 x 160 mm, 8⅝ x 6¼ in. Dated above, in the artist's hand, 1489. Monogram and cross in an unknown hand.

Coll. v. Praun (Nuremberg, see Heller, p. 87) Pacetti (Lugt 2057). Esterhazy and Posonyi-Hulot. Acquired 1877. KdZ 2.

BIBLIOGRAPHY: Lippmann, no. 2; Friedländer-Bock, p. 21; Tietze, no. 4; Flechsig, II, p. 381; Winkler, *Zeichnungen*, no. 18; Panofsky, no. 1220; Winkler, *Altdeutsche Zeichnungen*, p. 14; Id., *Dürer*, pp. 14 ff.

This page invites comparison with two other drawings of the same subject: *The Cavalcade* (W.16, formerly in Bremen) and *Horsemen Fighting* (W.17, London). These three drawings provide examples of Dürer's art at the end of his apprenticeship. The soldiers portrayed here are probably those at the foot of the Cross. The drawing was engraved in 1780 by M. C. Prestel, when it was still in the von Praun collection at Nuremberg.

19. *Couple on Horseback*

Pen and black ink, partially heightened with watercolor. Watermark: Gothic "p" with flower (variant of Briquet 8675). 215 x 165 mm, 8½ x 6½ in. Dated 1496 above and inscribed with monogram below by an unknown hand.

Coll. Andreossy and Posonyi-Hulot. Acquired 1877. KdZ 3.

BIBLIOGRAPHY: Lippmann, no. 3; Friedländer-Bock, p. 22; Tietze, p. 48; Flechsig,

II, p. 61; Winkler, *Zeichnungen*, no. 54; Panofsky, no. 1246; Winkler, *Dürer*, pp. 36, 38.

The authenticity of this drawing has often been questioned. Mr. and Mrs. Tietze do not believe it to be by Dürer, whereas Panofsky considers it a copy, or else a copy by the artist of one of his earlier works. Panofsky is here in closer agreement with Flechsig, who views this work as the definitive drawing, which would have been preceded by a sketch. There are close similarities between our drawing and Dürer's woodcut *Knight and Lansquenet* (B.131), particularly in the dog, the caparison of the horse, and the tree at the left. Winkler agrees with this, insofar as he would date the drawing before the print. The dating varies between the years 1492-93 and 1495-96. The theme was influenced by similar pieces by the Housebook Master—an argument for placing its execution sometime during Dürer's years of travel. A date between 1492 and the beginning of 1494 seems most plausible.

20. *St. Catherine (kneeling to the left)*

Pen and black ink. 234 x 167 mm, 9¼ x 6½ in. Signed below with Dürer's monogram in an unknown hand.

Coll. Basan (Lugt 221), Desperet (Lugt 721), Firmin-Didot (Lugt 119), and Heyl (Lugt 2879). Acquired 1922. KdZ 11 765.

BIBLIOGRAPHY: Lippmann, no. 627; Tietze, no. 81; Flechsig, II, p. 404; Winkler, *Zeichnungen*, no. 74; Panofsky, no. 852; Winkler, *Dürer*, p. 108.

Dufresne published an engraving made after this drawing in the *Receuil de 120 sujets . . . dont les originaux font partie de la collection du Sr. Basan père* (pl. 32, nos. 51-53). R. Schilling (in *St J* 1, 1929, p. 123) was the first to discover this engraving. The drawing dates from Dürer's first visit to Venice in 1494-95, as shown by the typically Venetian costume of the saint. Flechsig is alone in considering this drawing to have been executed after Dürer's return. There is another study of a St. Catherine (W.73) in Cologne, dating from the Venetian trip, that is sometimes thought to be a study after a painting, while the Berlin work is most likely to be an original creation by the artist.

21. *The Quarry*

Watercolor. Watermark: crown. 214 x 168 mm, 8⅜ x 6⅝ in. Signed upper right by an unknown hand and dated 1510.

Coll. J. D. Böhm (Lugt 1442), Hausmann (Lugt 378), and Blasius. Acquired 1935. KdZ 15 338.

BIBLIOGRAPHY: Lippmann, no. 139; Tietze, no. 440; Flechsig, II, pp. 75, 302; Winkler, *Zeichnungen*, no. 111; Panofsky, no. 1395; Winkler, *Altdeutsche Zeichnungen*, pp. 31 ff.; Id., *Dürer*, p. 72.

Dürer made a group of studies (W.106-111) of a quarry near Nuremberg (perhaps the Schmausenbuck, which still exists today near that city). These drawings in different media (pen, watercolor, or gouache) were probably executed after his return from Venice between 1495 and 1497. This drawing from the group was used as a model by the artist in 1513, with variations, for the landscape in the engraving *Knight, Death, and the Devil* (B.98). We owe the date, generally accepted today, to Flechsig's research. Previously the date inscribed on the drawing was believed to be correct.

22. *Valley near Kalchreuth*

Watercolor and gouache. Watermark: ox head and flower (variant of Briquet 14871-14874). 103 x 316 mm, 4 x 12½ in. Signed with a monogram in the upper portion probably by Hans von Kulmbach.

Coll. Festetits, J. D. Böhm (Lugt 1442) and Posonyi-Hulot. Acquired 1877. KdZ 5.

BIBLIOGRAPHY: Lippmann, no. 14; Friedländer-Bock, p. 29; Tietze, no. 592; Flechsig, II, p. 139; Winkler, *Zeichnungen*, no. 117; Panofsky, no. 1397; Winkler, *Dürer*, p. 87.

Dürer drew the landscape to the north of the village of Kalchreuth, with the plateau of Honings and the Village of Hetzles, from almost the same vantage point as the watercolor that was formerly in Bremen (W.118). (O. Mitius, a Nuremberg specialist in local history, identified the view.) These two watercolors are among the best of Dürer's early landscapes. The Berlin catalogue places its drawing in 1514, although Pauli had earlier proposed a date between 1495 and 1500 (Dürer exhibition in the Kunsthalle, Bremen, 1911). Today, in general, the date favored is around 1500.

23. *Angel Playing a Lute*

Silverpoint, heightened with white on tinted gray-violet paper. 268 x 196 mm, 10½ x 7¾ in. Above, monogram and date 1497.

Coll. Lawrence, Woodburn, Coningham (Lugt 476), Hawkins and Mitchell. Acquired 1890. KdZ 3877.

BIBLIOGRAPHY: Lippmann, no. 73; Friedländer-Bock, p. 24; Tietze, no. 124; Flechsig, II, p. 286; Winkler, *Zeichnungen*, no. 144; Panofsky, no. 869; Winkler, *Dürer*, pp. 89, 110.

This is the first drawing to which we can be certain that Dürer himself affixed his famous monogram. From the technical point of view it invites comparison with drawings W.143 (formerly in the Balsius collection) and W.286 (London). As the numerous changes show, the angel is a life study that the artist completed by adding wings, wall, and white highlights. Its resemblance to the angels in the *Apocalypse* has often been noted. According to Flechsig the same model, probably an apprentice of the artist, was also used for the male profile head in Frankfurt (W. 287).

24. *Male Nude Fighting a Dragon (Hercules?)*

Pen and brown ink. 195 x 190 mm, 7⅝ x 7½ in. Strip of paper added at the bottom. Damaged area betwen the head and the club. Scrawled monogram.

Coll. Posonyi-Hulot. Acquired 1877. KdZ 6.

BIBLIOGRAPHY: Lippmann, no. 9; Friedländer-Bock, p. 23; Tietze, no. A 52; Winkler, *Zeichnungen*, no. 156; Panofsky, no. 913; Winkler, *Dürer*, p. 95; L. Oehler in *MJKW* 17, 1955, pp. 134 ff.

Dürer's authorship of this work has often been questioned. However, in spite of certain weaknesses in the drawing, there do not seem to be sufficient grounds for removing it from his oeuvre. Winkler dates the drawing from the period of the *Apocalypse*. J. Meder (in *JKSAK* 30, 1910, pp. 219 ff.) has described the evolution of the theme of the kneeling man, from antiquity to Dürer.

25. *Faun*

Pen and brown ink. 262 x 156 mm, 10¼ x 6⅛ in.

Coll. Crozat (Lugt 474). Acquired 1924. KdZ 11 922.

BIBLIOGRAPHY: Lippmann, no. 676; Tietze, A 55; Flechsig, II, p. 422; Winkler, *Zeichnungen*, no. 157; Panofsky, no. 929; Winkler, *Dürer*, p. 95.

Winkler believes this drawing, probably based on an Italian model, to be closely related to the engraving *Jealousy* (B.73). The similarity exists as much in the satyr, seated at the left, as in the standing Hercules to the right. Also the highly accomplished linear style links it to the engravings of the end of the 1490's.

26. *Three Peasants and a Peasant Couple*

Pen and black-brown ink. 190 x 223 mm, 7 ½ x 8 ¾ in. Two vertical folds in the paper separate the groups. Signed with a monogram in the center by Dürer (?).

Coll. Andréossy and Lawrence (Lugt 2445). Acquired 1903. Kdz 4270.

BIBLIOGRAPHY: Lippmann, no. 665; Friedländer-Bock, p. 24; Tietze, no. W 11; Flechsig, II, p. 416; Winkler, *Zeichnungen*, no. 164; Panofsky, no. 1237; Winkler, *Dürer*, pp. 90, 98.

This group of three figures was used again by Dürer, with a few changes, in his engraving *Three Peasants* (B.86), while the group at the right reappears in the engraving *Peasant and His Wife*. According to Winkler the group at the left is a study after nature, while the pair to the right was added from memory. Panofsky views this study as a working drawing based upon other studies after nature and is somewhat dubious about its authenticity. Finally, the Tietzes consider the page to be a workshop product. As Winkler explains it, the faint lines of the preliminary sketch, still visible throughout, point to an original work. It is not at all certain, however, that it is a study after nature like the *Angel Playing a Lute* (cat. 23). This drawing may be a free invention of the artist as is the *Three Lansquenets* (cat. 18). Panofsky's and the Tietzes' negative attitude is apparently based on the inferior quality of the drawing of the group at the right. Neither the character of the drawing nor the ink, however, admit the conclusion of a much later date or another hand. Winkler gives 1498 as the date for the two corresponding engravings.

27. *Forest Spring with St. Paul and St. Anthony*

Pen and black ink. 186 x 185 mm, 7 ¼ x 7 ¼ in. Signed below with a monogram in an unknown hand.

Coll. Drexler and v. Klinkosch (Lugt 577). Acquired 1890. KdZ 3867.

BIBLIOGRAPHY: Lippmann, no. 440; Friedländer-Bock, p. 24; Tietze, no. 272; Flechsig, II, pp. 353 ff.; Winkler, *Zeichnungen*, no. 182; Panofsky, no. 866; Winkler, *Altdeutsche Zeichnungen*, pp. 32 ff.; Id., *Dürer*, p. 123.

This drawing may be the preliminary sketch for the woodcut *St. Anthony and St. Paul*. The idea of this drawing is further elaborated in the version now in the Germanisches Nationalmuseum, Nuremberg (formerly in the Blasius collection, Brunswick, W.183), where the figures comprise the principal part of the composition. The highly finished rendering of the forest places the Berlin drawing in the vicinity of Dürer's pure landscape studies (see W.109). The woodcut should probably be placed around 1502 and the drawing slightly earlier.

28. *Lansquenet Seen from the Back*

Pen and black ink. 277 x 173 mm, 4 x 6¾ in. Signed above with monogram by the artist.

Coll. Gelosi (Lugt 513) and Dupan (Lugt 1440). Acquired 1926. KdZ 12 307.

BIBLIOGRAPHY: Lippmann, no. 677; Tietze, no. A 53; Flechsig, II, p. 423; Winkler, *Zeichnungen*, no. 253; Panofsky, no. 1231.

H. and E. Tietze continue to attribute this drawing to Hans Schäufelein. Panofsky is dubious about assigning it to Dürer. Neither Schäufelein nor Kulmbach, however, would have been capable of creating such taut figures. At this time no known German draftsman, with the exception of Dürer, could have created so extraordinary a drawing. Dürer alone, with a technique that combined elegance and power, drew similar silhouettes of lansquenets. We must imagine that studies for the executioner in the woodcut of *The Martyrdom of St. Catherine* (B.120), for the lansquenets in the *Ecce Homo* (B.91), and for *The Bearing of the Cross* for the *Great Passion* looked very similar.

29. *Portrait of Willibald Pirckheimer*

Silverpoint. 211 x 150 mm, 8¼ x 5⅞ in. Upper right edge, Dürer's monogram, preceded by "᾽Αρσενος τῇ ψωλη ἐς τον πρωχτόν." Lower right, another Dürer monogram (added later).

Coll. Blasius. Acquired 1951. KdZ 24 623.

BIBLIOGRAPHY: Lippmann, no. 142; Tietze, no. 219; Flechsig, II, p. 302; Winkler, *Zeichnungen*, no. 268; Panofsky, no. 1036; Winkler, *Dürer*, p. 179.

This drawing is the preparatory study for the large charcoal portrait of 1503 (see cat. 30). The Greek inscription was probably added by Pirckheimer at the same time as the monogram. Flechsig, however, dates this drawing 1504-05, later than the charcoal portrait.

30. *Profile Portrait of Willibald Pirckheimer*

Charcoal, lightly heightened with white under the eye and on the forehead. 281 x 208 mm, 11 x 8⅛ in. Dated lower left 1503.

Coll. Imhoff, Zoomer (Lugt 1511) and Defer-Dumesmil (Lugt 739). Acquired 1901. KdZ 4230.

BIBLIOGRAPHY: Lippmann, no. 376; Friedländer-Bock, p. 25; Tietze, no. 220; Flechsig, II, p. 302; Winkler, *Zeichnungen*, no. 270; Panofsky, no. 1037; Winkler, *Altdeutsche Zeichnungen*, pp. 22 ff.; Id., *Dürer*, p. 179.

53

This drawing was based on the silverpoint study (see cat. 29), but in this work Dürer made several changes, notably in the areas of the mouth, eye, and cap. On the verso there is a notation by Pirckheimer's grandson, Willibald Imhoff the Elder: "Meynes Anherrenn Wilbalden pirkaimers Seligenn Abcontrafectur durch Albrecht dürer 1503." In the private account book of the Imhoff family, this drawing is mentioned along with another portrait, also in charcoal, of Pirckheimer's wife. These two drawings were sold in 1633, along with some others, to a Dutch painter and art dealer, A. Bloemaert. Panofsky believes, following Habich, that this charcoal drawing was conceived as a study for a medal, as seems indicated by the placement of the profile, which was rare for Dürer at this period. Panofsky related this work to the medal of 1517 (Albrecht Dürer, "Des Meisters Gemälde, Kupferstiche und Holzschnitte," *Klassiker der Kunst*, 4th ed., F. Winkler, p. 402).

31. *Annunciation*

Pen and brown ink with watercolor. 312 x 204 mm, 12¼ x 8 in. Signed below with monogram, beneath which is inscribed "um ein pfund," and dated in the right corner 1503.

Coll. Denon (Lugt 779). Acquired 1894. KdZ 4005.

BIBLIOGRAPHY: Lippmann, no. 442; Friedländer-Bock, p. 25; Tietze, no. 263; Flechsig, II, p. 354; Winkler, *Zeichnungen*, no. 291; Panofsky, no. 507; Winkler, *Dürer*, pp. 152 ff.

The drawing is very closely related to the corresponding woodcut for the *Life of the Virgin* (B.83). It is generally agreed, however, that the drawing was not conceived as a study for the engraving. The inscription "for a pound" leads us to suppose that the drawing was meant to be sold, or to serve as a model for a painting commission (for the price of a pound). The architecture was rigorously drawn with the aid of a ruler and compass and is clearly based upon Italian models. In the years following 1500 Dürer was concerned with the representation of the human figure within an interior. The series of woodcuts for the *Life of the Virgin* bears witness to this concern.

32. *The Birth of the Virgin*

Pen and black ink. 288 x 213 mm, 11⅜ x 8⅜ in. Signed with monogram by an unknown hand in the lower right.

Coll. His de la Salle (Lugt 1333) and Posonyi-Hulot (Lugt 2041). Acquired 1877. KdZ 7.

BIBLIOGRAPHY: Lippmann, no. 7; Friedländer-Bock, no. 25; Tietze, no. 207; Flechsig, II, p. 267; Winkler, *Zeichnungen*, no. 292; Panofsky, no. 506; Winkler, *Dürer*, pp. 152, 156.

This drawing is the first preliminary study for the corresponding woodcut in the *Life of the Virgin* (B.80) and already contains all the principal elements of the print. The latter, however, was elaborated by the addition of several figures and its composition completed by adding an angel in the upper third of the page. The Tietzes quite rightly observed the Italianate elements in the furnishings. On the verso (not illustrated) is a small pen and ink sketch of the Crucifixion.

33. *The Arrest of Christ*

Pen and brownish-black ink. Watermark: Gothic "p" with flower (variant of Briquet no. 8675). 253 x 202 mm, 10 x 8 in. Scrawled monogram below.

Original collection. KdZ 74.

BIBLIOGRAPHY: Lippmann, no. 33; Friedländer-Bock, p. 24; Tietze, no. A 47; Flechsig, II, p. 279; Winkler, *Zeichnungen*, no. 318; Panofsky, no. 1125; L. Oehler in *MJKW* 17, 1955, pp. 141 ff.; *Meister um Albrecht Dürer*, no. 401.

This very sketchy study is often related to Dürer's *Green Passion* in the Albertina (W.298-317). The authenticity of the two works—the drawing as well as the *Green Passion*—has often been challenged without producing decisive arguments against their attribution to Dürer. The drawing obviously constitutes the preliminary sketch for the corresponding composition in the *Green Passion*, and also has specific similarities to the painting of the same subject, in Darmstadt, generally considered an early work by Dürer. Here, as in the painting, we see the same resigned expression of the Savior and again find the soldier who strikes Christ from behind. The corresponding page of the *Green Passion* shows, as does the Darmstadt work, the soldier seizing the hem of Christ's robe (Winkler, *Dürer*, pl. 14). Other motifs from the drawing appear, as Winkler has shown, in the artist's graphic works of the same period. All these observations argue in favor of the authenticity both of the drawing and of the *Green Passion*.

34. *Drapery Studies*

Brush and black ink, heightened with white on brown tinted paper. Watermark: crenellated tower. 271 x 265 mm, 10⅝ x 10⅜ in.

Coll. Posonyi-Hulot. Acquired 1877. KdZ 32.

BIBLIOGRAPHY: Lippmann, no. 69; Friedländer-Bock, p. 34; Tietze, no. A 251; Winkler, *Zeichnungen*, no. 340; Panofsky, no. 1467; Winkler, *Altdeutsche Zeichnungen*, pp. 35 ff.; Id., *Dürer*, p. 177.

This drawing originally formed part of the same sheet as the two studies now in Vienna (W.338/339). Winkler relates these studies to the drawing of *The Coronation of the Virgin* in London (W.337). But the two silhouettes of the drawing shown here rather suggest the Virgin of Mercy of a Last Judgment, or the Virgin of Lamentation.

Several scholars have expressed serious doubts concerning the attribution of this drawing to Dürer. The study of hands in Vienna (W.338) in particular seems to show few of the qualities characteristic of Dürer. In any case these drawings certainly belong to the Dürer circle. The technique of tinting the paper places this drawing in the vicinity of the studies for the *Four Apostles* (cat. 55). Winkler, however, dates these works between the years 1503 and 1505.

35. *Portrait of an Architect*

Brush, in black and white on blue Venetian paper. Watermark: Cardinal's hat (Briquet 3391). 386 x 263 mm, 15⅛ x 10⅜ in. Monogram and date 1506.

Coll. Andreossy and Gigoux (Lugt 1164). Acquired 1882. KdZ 2274.

BIBLIOGRAPHY: Lippmann, no. 10; Friedländer-Bock, p. 26; Tietze, no. 313; Flechsig, II, p. 268; Winkler, *Zeichnungen*, no. 382; Panofsky, no. 738; Winkler, *Dürer*, p. 194.

This page is one of the keystones of Dürer's drawing. It is one of the studies for the painting *The Feast of the Rose Garlands* (National Museum, Prague), which Dürer painted for the chapel of the German merchants church during his second Venetian visit. The person portrayed, who in the painting kneels at the right-hand border, has been most often identified as Jerome of Augsburg, the architect of the Fondaco de'Tedeschi. This identification seems logical, although no proof of it has ever been established.

36. *Female Nude with a Shield (Study in Proportions)*

Pen and ink, background painted black-brown. 303 x 206 mm, 12 x 8 in.

Coll. Posonyi-Hulot. Acquired 1877. KdZ 44.

BIBLIOGRAPHY: Lippmann, no. 37; Friedländer-Bock, p. 24; Tietze, no. 174; Flechsig, II, pp. 104 ff.; Winkler, no. 414; Panofsky, no. 1634.

Dürer outlined the nude on the recto of the drawing and filled in the contours on the verso. He then proceeded with the drawing as usual. Winkler, following Flechsig, dates the series of proportion studies (W.410-428), of which this is one, around 1506, at the time of Dürer's second Italian trip. Panofsky, however, has definitely proved that the entire series, with the exception of the studies for the Eve in the Madrid painting, must have been executed around 1500.

37. *Kneeling Apostle*

Brush and black ink, heightened with white on green tinted paper. 352 x 276 mm, 13⅞ x 10⅞ in. Signed and dated 1508.

Coll. Andreossy and Gigoux (Lugt 1164). Acquired 1882. KdZ 2273.

BIBLIOGRAPHY: Lippmann, no. 22; Friedländer-Bock, p. 26; Tietze, no. 373; Flechsig, II, p. 273; Winkler, *Zeichnungen*, no. 454; Panofsky, no. 486; Winkler, *Dürer*, p. 204.

Study for the robes of the apostle kneeling at the left of the Heller altar. Nine letters of Dürer dated from 1507 to 1508 provide documentation for the history of the altarpiece, which was commissioned by the Frankfurt merchant Jacob Heller. In the contract Dürer agreed to paint the central panel himself. The altarpiece was delivered in August 1509 in Frankfurt-on-Main, where the work was placed in the Dominican church. In 1615 the central panel of the polyptich was sold by the Frankfurt Dominicans to Duke Maximilian of Bavaria. The work was destroyed by a fire in the Munich Episcopal Residence on August 9 or 10, 1674. The Dominicans had meanwhile procured a copy of the work by Jobst Harich to replace the original. This copy, as well as a better-preserved drawing after the central panel (Winkler, *Dürer*, fig. 99), permits a reconstruction of the compositional elements. The central panel depicted the apostles grouped around the empty tomb of the Virgin, with the coronation of the Virgin above. In the center background the artist painted his self-portrait, holding a tablet which bears his signature. Numerous studies of apostles' heads as well as studies of drapery and hands (W.448-65) have survived. All were executed with brush on green tinted paper, as in the Berlin drawing.

38. *Samson Conquering the Philistines*

Pen and brush with black ink, heightened with white on blue-gray tinted paper. Rounded above. Watermark: serpent (Briquet no. 13807/8). 321 x 156 mm, 12⅝ x 6⅛ in. Signed in the cartouche below: "Albertus Dürer Norenbergensis faciebat, post. virginis. partum. 1510," with monogram.

Coll. Imhoff(?), Andreossy, Pourtalès, and Posonyi-Hulot. Acquired 1877. KdZ 18.

BIBLIOGRAPHY: Lippmann, no. 24; Friedländer-Bock, p. 27; Tietze, no. W. 78; Flechsig, II, pp. 273-275; Winkler, *Zeichnungen*, no. 486; Panofsky, no. 1538; Winkler, *Dürer*, p. 248.

This page is a reworking of a drawing with the same theme. In 1510 Dürer delivered three designs for reliefs of the Fugger tombs in the Church of St. Anne in Augsburg. (These projects were, however, only to be executed after 1520 by the Augsburg sculptor Adolf Daucher.) In the lower portion of these long, narrow areas, rounded above, Dürer portrayed either a dead man entombed or a sarcophagus in the style of the early Florentine Renaissance. In the space above these representations the artist depicted *Samson Conquering the Philistines* (W.483), *Samson at the Gates of Gaza* (W.484), and the *Ascension* (W.485). The only original study of these on green paper to have survived is the project for the first scene. Of the two other projects only two preparatory sketches in pen and ink remain. These compositions, which Dürer felt to be particularly successful, were later repeated with slight variations. In order to differentiate them from the commissioned works, the pages of the second version, *Samson Conquering the Philistines* and the *Resurrection of Christ* (W.487, Vienna, Albertina), were executed on tinted blue-gray paper. In the later versions Dürer omitted allusions to the dead and symbols of death and provided these works with a detailed signature. Tietze and Panofsky consider these two pages to be studio copies, but the character of the inscription proves Dürer's collaboration. Winkler has shown, with good reason moreover, that the nature of the changes made in the drawings unquestionably points to a Dürer authorship. The detailed inscription on the cartouche, in both the Vienna and Berlin drawings, confirms this theory.

39. *The Rest on the Flight into Egypt*

Pen and brown ink. 277 x 207 mm, 10⅞ x 8⅛ in. Signed with monogram and date 1511 in the upper left.

Coll. Le Levre, Festetits (Lugt 926) and v. Klinkosch (Lugt 577). Acquired 1890. KdZ 3866.

BIBLIOGRAPHY: Lippmann, no. 513; Friedländer-Bock, p. 28; Tietze, no. 462; Flechsig, II, p. 355; Winkler, *Zeichnungen*, no. 513; Panofsky, no. 517; Winkler, *Altdeutsche Zeichnungen*, p. 19; Id., *Dürer*, p. 245.

This page sketched with prodigious sureness of touch is a masterpiece among Dürer drawings, at this moment reaching a peak of maturity. With this drawing begins a long series of depictions of the Virgin that Dürer made in the second decade of the sixteenth century. H. Beenken (in *ZDVKW* 3, 1936, pp. 91 ff.) finds motifs borrowed from *The Virgin and Child with St. Anne* by Leonardo (Louvre), whereas Panofsky proposes a more general Italian influence. But any real justification in speaking of influences is questionable when confronted by such a direct and spontaneous sketch, where each line, including the monogram and the date, has its specific function in the composition.

40. *Virgin and Child on a Crescent Moon*

Pen and brown ink. 155 x 110 mm, 6⅛ x 4⅜ in. Monogram and date 1514.

Coll. Paignon-Dijonval. Acquired 1909. KdZ 4415.

BIBLIOGRAPHY: Lippmann, no. 795; Friedländer-Bock, p. 29; Tietze, no. 595; Flechsig, II, pp. 582 ff.; Winkler, *Zeichnungen*, no. 530; Panofsky, no. 703; Winkler, *Dürer*, p. 246.

Between 1511 and 1515 Dürer was particularly drawn to the theme of the Virgin and Child, which he developed in several different contexts. In 1514 he made pen and ink drawings of this theme in ever new variations.

Flechsig has suggested a classification for these sheets. A copy of the Berlin drawing is in Oxford.

41. *Portrait of a Young Girl*

Charcoal. 420 x 290 mm, 16½ x 11⅜ in. Signed above with a monogram and the date 1515.

Coll. Andreossy and Posonyi-Hulot. Acquired 1877. KdZ 24.

BIBLIOGRAPHY: Lippmann, no. 46; Friedländer-Bock, p. 29; Tietze, no. 642; Flechsig, II, p. 280; Winkler, *Zeichnungen*, no. 562; Panofsky, no. 1109; Winkler, *Dürer*, p. 267.

With the great charcoal *Portrait of the Artist's Mother* (W.559), dated 1514, a new and monumental portrait style appeared in Dürer's work. This portrait of a young girl is generally considered with another drawing, also dated 1515, now in Stockholm (W.561). Attempts to identify the two girls as relatives of the artist have failed for lack of comparative elements.

42. *St. Catherine, Seated*

Pen and black-brown ink. Watermark: anchor in a circle with flower. 251 x 184 mm, 9⅞ x 7¼ in. Monogram inscribed by an unknown hand at the lower right.

Acquired 1881. KdZ 2361.

BIBLIOGRAPHY: Lippmann, no. 42; Friedländer-Bock, p. 30; Tietze, no. 737; Flechsig, II, p. 280; Winkler, *Zeichnungen*, no. 595; Panofsky, no. 855.

This freely drawn work, of which several copies exist, clearly shows how Dürer's sense of form evolved in the spirit of the High Renaissance, particularly when compared to the St. Catherine of 1494-95 (cat. 20). The dating varies between 1514 and 1518, with the later date agreed on by the majority of scholars today.

43. *Woman Seated on a Bench*

Pen and brown ink. Watermark: fragment of an ox head. 218 x 167 mm, 8½ x 6½ in. Signed with monogram and dated 1514 above, in an unknown hand.

Coll. Vallardi and Mitchell. Acquired 1890. KdZ 3876.

BIBLIOGRAPHY: Lippmann, no. 79; Friedländer-Bock, p. 29; Tietze, no. 582; Flechsig, II, pp. 287 ff.; Winkler, *Zeichnungen*, no. 621; Panofsky, no. 1273.

Dürer freely used this study from nature as a point of departure for the figure of Melancholy in his famous engraving of 1514 (B.74).

44. *Ornament for Armor*

Pen and brown ink. 208 x 260 mm, 8⅛ x 10¼ in. Monogram inscribed in the upper part by an unknown hand.

Coll. Posonyi-Hulot. Acquired 1877. KdZ 29.

BIBLIOGRAPHY: Lippmann, no. 50; Friedländer-Bock, p. 30; Tietze, no. 682; Flechsig, II, p. 109; Winkler, *Zeichnungen*, no. 681; Panofsky, no. 1452; Winkler, *Dürer*, p. 284.

According to P. Post (in *ZHWKK* n.s. 6, 1939, p. 253) this drawing, along with pages W.678-680 and 682, forms part of the project for the decoration of the silvered armor commissioned by the Emperor Maximilian I from the celebrated Augsburg armorer Koloman Helmschmied. Although the armor was completed before the Emperor's death financial difficulties made him unable to accept delivery. The identification of this study as the upper rim of a thigh guard, suggested by several specialists, is not wholly convincing. Nor can we be certain that it was intended for the decoration of a shoulder plate or a helmet. Dürer's talents as a decorator are fully displayed here in the light and free play of pen and ink, as in the drawings for the Emperor's prayer book (Munich and Besançon).

45. *Two Designs for Jewelry*

Pen and brown-black ink. 93 x 62 mm, 3⅝ x 2½ in.

Coll. v. Lanna (Lugt 2773). Acquired 1910. KdZ 4453.

BIBLIOGRAPHY: Lippmann, no. 907; Friedländer-Bock, p. 30; Tietze, no. 680; Flechsig, II, no. 476; Winkler, *Zeichnungen*, no. 733; Panofsky, no. 1577; Winkler, *Altdeutsche Zeichnungen*, pp. 37 ff.

Here we can see the lessons which Dürer received from his father vividly recalled in his own designs for metalwork, jewelry, vases, and medallions. In this drawing Dürer was able to give full expression to his taste for ornament, just as in the drawings made almost at the same time for the Emperor's prayer book and for the armor decoration (cat. 44).

46. *Portrait of a Mechelen Goldsmith*

Pen and brown ink. 159 x 101 mm, 6¼ x 4 in. Bears monogram and date, as well as inscription by Dürer: "ein goltschmit von mechell zw antorff gemacht."

Coll. Lawrence (inv. 2445). Acquired 1894. KdZ 4009.

BIBLIOGRAPHY: Lippmann, no. 445; Friedländer-Bock, p. 31; Tietze, no. 773; Flechsig, II, pp. 208, 210, 237; J. Duverger, "Conrat Meijt" (Royal Academy of Belgium, Beaux-Arts class, *Mémoires*, 2nd ser., vol. 5, fasc. 2 ff., 1934, p. 25 and note 1); Winkler, *Zeichnungen*, no. 745; Panofsky, no. 1072.

In his journal Dürer mentions the goldsmith Stefan Capello, whose chalk portrait he made (now in Amsterdam, W.812). There is a definite resemblance between the people portrayed in the Amsterdam and Berlin drawings, but the latter cannot be identified with any degree of certainty as Capello. J. Duverger also mentions the Mechelen goldsmith, M. Desabliaux, who in the company of Conrat Meit made Dürer's acquaintance in Antwerp. This page forms part of a pen and ink sketchbook (see cat. 47).

47. *Portrait of Paul Topler and Martin Pfinzing*

Silverpoint. 128 x 190 mm, 5 x 7½ in. Inscription by Dürer at the upper left: "pawll dopler 1520 LXI jor altt"; and at the right: "mertn pfintzing XX jor alt"; below that: "zw ach gemacht." Dürer's monogram signed at the right of each headdress.

Coll. Sandrart, Denon, Lawrence (Lugt 2445), Holford (Lugt 2243), and v. Weissbach (Lugt 25396). Acquired 1900. KdZ 4179.

BIBLIOGRAPHY: Lippmann, no. 439; Friedländer-Bock, p. 31; Tietze, no. 766; Flechsig, II, pp. 37, 212, 216; Winkler, *Zeichnungen*, no. 761; Panofsky, 1482; Winkler, *Dürer*, pp. 295, 300.

During his journey to the Netherlands Dürer used two small sketchbooks: one for pen and ink drawings and another, with tinted pages, for silverpoint drawings. Of the latter fifteen leaves survive, whose versos have been frequently used as well. In all, twenty-seven silverpoint drawings have been preserved. This depiction of two Nurembergers (its extraordinary finesse made it an early subject of admiration) was possibly the beginning of the notebook for silverpoint. The portraits were executed at the time of Dürer's visit to Aachen for the coronation of Charles V (October 23, 1520). Dürer expressly noted in his journal, between October 7 and 23: "Ich hab Paulus Topler und Merten Pfinzing in mein büchlein conterfet" (I have drawn portraits of Paulus Topler and Martin Pfinzing in my notebook).

48. *Portrait of Lazarus Ravensburger with the Tower of the Court of Liere in Antwerp*

Silverpoint. 112 x 169 mm, 4⅜ x 6⅝ in. Inscription by Dürer at the upper left: "... rus rafenspurger ... gemacht zw antorff."

Coll. Lugt 2882 and Firmin-Didot (Lugt 119). Acquired 1877. KdZ 35.

BIBLIOGRAPHY: Lippmann, no. 55; Friedländer-Bock, p. 31; Tietze, no. 782; Flechsig, II, pp. 217 ff.; Winkler, *Zeichnungen*, no. 774; Panofsky, no. 1480; Winkler, *Altdeutsche Zeichnungen*, pp. 26 ff.; Id., *Dürer*, p. 300.

Lazarus Ravensburger, from 1517 on Lisbon agent of the Augsburg firm of Höchstetter, is mentioned several times in Dürer's journal. The artist made him a gift of a St. Jerome and three books of woodcuts (*The Apocalypse*, the *Large Passion*, and the *Life of the Virgin*), and in 1520 did his portrait. The Berlin drawing may be a replica made for personal reasons. The tower has been identified by J. Veth and S. Müller (*Albrecht Dürers Niederländische Reise*, 1918, vol. 2, p. 264). On the verso (not illustrated) there are two young girls in Netherlandish costume. Like the preceding drawing this work belongs to the sketchbook in silverpoint, used during the artist's trip to the Netherlands.

49. *Head of an Old Man of 93*

Brush and black ink, heightened with white on tinted dark mauve paper. 269 x 200 mm, 10⅝ x 7⅞ in. Bears the monogram and date 1521 at the upper left.

Coll. Woodburn, Trier, Esterhazy, and Posonyi-Hulot. Acquired 1877. KdZ 38.

BIBLIOGRAPHY: Lippmann, no. 61; Friedländer-Bock, p. 40; Tietze, no. 805; Flechsig, II, p. 329; Winkler, *Zeichnungen*, no. 789; Panofsky, no. 819; Winkler, *Altdeutsche Zeichnungen*, p. 26; Id., *Dürer*, p. 307.

The authenticity of this drawing has only been questioned once, by E. Bock in the Berlin catalogue. The old man portrayed here is the same one who appears in the famous Vienna drawing (W.788), but a relationship between the works cannot be established with any certainty. Generally the Berlin drawing is considered to be later than the one in Vienna. Winkler nonetheless feels that the Berlin drawing is closer to the original study than the Vienna work, probably a drawing in chalk or charcoal. The two drawings, as well as a study of arms (W.790), a desk with books (W.791), and a skull (W.792), are preparatory studies for the *St. Jerome* in Lisbon.

50. *Study Sheet with Nine Depictions of St. Christopher*

Pen and black ink. Watermark: fleur de lis with flower and "A" (Briquet 1746). 228 x 407 mm, 9 x 16 in. Monogram and date 1521 above.

Coll. Andreossy and Duval. Acquired 1910. KdZ 4477.

BIBLIOGRAPHY: Lippmann, no. 849; Friedländer-Bock, p. 32; Tietze, no. 877; Flechsig, II, p. 469; Winkler, *Zeichnungen*, no. 800; Panofsky, no. 801; Winkler, *Dürer*, pp. 309, 327.

This drawing is connected to a notation in Dürer's travel notebooks to the Netherlands, according to which he executed four projects for a St. Christopher for Joachim Patenir. The drawings in London (W.801) and Besançon (W.802) are most probably part of this series. As L. Baldass has shown (in *Die Graphischen Künste*, vol. 51, 1928, pp. 23 ff.), the silhouette of St. Christopher in the chiaroscuro drawing by Patenir, now in the Louvre, was based on the preliminary sketch for the Berlin drawing. This page perfectly illustrates Dürer's own words when he claimed that a good painter is "voller figur," that is, overflowing with creative imagination.

51. *Portrait of a Young Man*

Brown and black charcoal or chalk. 361 x 258 mm, 14¼ x 10⅛ in. Upper edge and upper corners cut. Monogram and date 1520 on upper margin.

Coll. Robinson (Lugt inv. 1433). Acquired 1880. KdZ 60.

BIBLIOGRAPHY: Lippmann, no. 50; Friedländer-Bock, p. 32; Tietze, no. 784; Flechsig, II, pp. 228, 230-32; Winkler, *Zeichnungen*, no. 804; Panofsky, no. 1071; Winkler, *Altdeutsche Zeichnungen*, p. 26; Id., *Dürer*, p. 302; *Deutsche Zeichnungen 1400-1900*, no. 63.

Flechsig identifies the sitter as the Portuguese Rodrigo Fernandez d'Almada, who is mentioned several times in Dürer's journal. However, the drawing bears no convincing resemblance to the portrait (W.813). Winkler considers this work to be one of the first of the large charcoal portraits which Dürer made in the Netherlands. As yet no one has been able to determine whether the artist used chalk or charcoal. Another unsolved problem is whether the brown lines on the sitter's hat and neck were drawn by Dürer or added later.

52. *Irish Soldiers and Peasants*

Pen and brown ink with watercolor. Watermark: coat of arms with a crown and three lilies. 210 x 282 mm, 8¼ x 11 in. Monogram with date 1521, with notation in Dürer's hand: "Also gand dy krigs man jn Irlandia hinder Engeland," at the right: "Allos gend dy pawern in Irlandyen."

Coll. Posonyi-Hulot. Acquired 1877. KdZ 37.

Bibliography: Lippmann, no. 62; Friedländer-Bock, p. 32; Tietze, no. 797; Flechsig, II, p. 234; Winkler, *Zeichnungen*, no. 824; Panofsky, no. 1293; Winkler, *Dürer*, p. 320.

This costume study belongs to the two drawings in the Louvre depicting Livonian women (W.826, 827). As is evident from the travel diaries of his trip to the Netherlands, Dürer was passionately interested in everything foreign. He noted, for example, having seen some pre-Columbian objects in Brussels. Dürer was not the only one of his times to be interested in rare and exotic costumes. Matthäus Schwarz, the Fugger treasurer in Augsburg, collected representations of antique costumes. It is difficult to understand Panofsky's view that Dürer, never having visited either Ireland or Livonia, must have copied these costume studies from other works. It is rather conceivable that Antwerp, already in those days an international, mercantile metropolis, had guests from all countries of Europe, and that Dürer might well have drawn them from life or memory. This drawing was probably based upon a preliminary sketch.

53. *St. Apollonia*

Black chalk on green tinted paper. Watermark: tall crown with cross (similar to Briquet 4895). 414 x 288 mm, 16¼ x 11⅜ in. Monogram and date 1521.

Coll. Robinson (Lugt 1433). Acquired 1880. KdZ 1527.

Bibliography: Lippmann, no. 65; Friedländer-Bock, p. 33; Tietze, no. 853; Flechsig, II, pp. 248, 284; Winkler, *Zeichnungen*, no. 846; Panofsky, 768; Winkler, *Dürer*, p. 322; *Deutsche Zeichnungen 1400-1900*, no. 65.

Immediately after his return from the Netherlands Dürer began work on a project for an altarpiece which was to show the Virgin enthroned between standing male and female saints. The identification of the Berlin study as St. Apollonia is based upon the presence of her attributes, tongs with a tooth, in the two compositional sketches in the Louvre and in Bayonne (W.838/839). Already in these two sketches we find the characteristically bowed head and lowered eyelids. Other large studies of the head for this altarpiece are in Paris (W.845), Milan (W.847), and London (W.848). Drapery studies for this work are divided among the collections of Hamburg (W.841), Nuremberg (formerly in the Blasius Coll., W.842), and Berlin (W.843/44). The study in Bremen was destroyed in 1945.

54. *Weeping Angel*

Black chalk, heightened with white on blue-gray tinted paper. 214 x 199 mm, 8½ x 7⅞ in. Monogram and date 1521 in the lower left.

Coll. Rogers and Breadalbane. Acquired 1886. KdZ 2879.

BIBLIOGRAPHY: Lippmann, no. 446; Friedländer-Bock, p. 32; Tietze, no. 868; Flechsig, II, p. 258; Winkler, *Zeichnungen*, no. 864; Panofsky, no. 543; Winkler, *Dürer*, p. 323.

This work, along with drawings W.858-863 and 865, is part of a group of preparatory studies for a large engraving of a Crucifixion with many figures, of which only the outlines of the composition were executed. The preliminary drawings are spread over the years 1521-23. In the engraving the Berlin study was used for the first angel at the left.

55. *Head of St. Mark*

Lead pencil, heightened with white on brown tinted paper. Watermark: bear (cf. Meder, Dürer catalog 85-95). 373 x 264 mm, 14⅝ x 10⅜ in. Somewhat trimmed down. Monogram and date 1526 at the lower right.

Coll. Andreossy, Lawrence, and Posonyi-Hulot. Acquired 1877. KdZ 46.

BIBLIOGRAPHY: Lippmann, no. 72; Friedländer-Bock, p. 34; Tietze, no. 952; Flechsig, II, p. 286; Winkler, *Zeichnungen*, no. 870; Panofsky, no. 830; Winkler, *Dürer*, p. 335; *Deutsche Zeichnungen 1400-1900*, no. 66.

Three studies of heads survive for the two panels, the *Four Apostles*, now in Munich. This *Head of St. Mark* is the most important. Dürer executed the Evangelist's head in a broad synthesis of forms, using a soft pencil on paper tinted with wide brush strokes. In spite of the strict forms of Dürer's late period, the drawing still has a pronounced calligraphic quality, especially evident in the rendering of the hair. The *Four Apostles*, which Dürer gave as a present to the City Council of Nuremberg in 1526, constitutes his vow of allegiance to the Reformation. Strictly speaking, the panels only depict three apostles (Peter, Paul, and John) toward whom advances the fourth, the Evangelist Mark. The history of the panels' genesis has been clarified by Panofsky (in *MJBK*, n.s. 8, 1931, pp. 18 ff.).

56. *Group for a Bearing of the Cross*

Pen and black ink, completed in places by lighter ink. 294 x 215 mm, 11½ x 8½ in. Inscribed at the right with monogram by an unknown hand.

Coll. Klinkosch (Lugt 577). Acquired 1890. KdZ 3868.

BIBLIOGRAPHY: Lippmann, no. 444; Friedländer-Bock, p. 34; Tietze, no. 922; Flechsig, I, p. 429, II, p. 355; Winkler, *Zeichnungen*, no. 893; Panofsky, no. 581; Winkler, *Dürer*, pp. 329, 344.

It is debatable whether this partial project for a Bearing of the Cross, showing only the group of thieves, is related to the drawing in Florence, dated 1520 (W.794), as stated by Panofsky. The Berlin drawing is more freely rendered than the series representing the Passion, which is oblong in format and was executed in the Netherlands (W.793-799). The two drawings W.794 and 893 are united into a single composition in the *grisaille* painting depicting the Bearing of the Cross. Three copies of this have survived (Dresden, Bergamo, and Richmond, Cook Coll.). All bear Dürer's monogram and the date 1527. It is now generally considered that this composition is not by Dürer, and it is doubtful whether the copies are after a lost work by the master.

PETER VISCHER THE YOUNGER

Sculptor, bronze caster, and draftsman. Second son of Peter Vischer the Elder, he was born in 1487 in Nuremberg, where he died in 1528.

57. *Virtutes et Voluptas*

Pen and brown ink with watercolor. 246 x 163 mm, 9⅝ x 4 in. Text on the verso.

Coll. v. Nagler (Lugt 2529). Acquired 1835. KdZ 1083.

58. *The Dream of Hercules*

Pen and brown ink with watercolor. 246 x 163 mm, 9⅝ x 6½ in. Text on the verso.

Coll. v. Nagler (Lugt 2529). Acquired 1835. KdZ 1082.

BIBLIOGRAPHY: E. W. Braun in *MKW* 8, 1915, pp. 52 ff.; H. Stierling in *MKW* 10, 1918, pp. 258 ff.; Friedländer-Bock, pp. 87 ff.; E. Schilling in *St J* 7/8, 1932, pp. 149 ff.; H. Röttinger, *Dürers Doppelgänger* (*Stud. z. deut. Kunstgesch.* 235), 1926, p. 229; S. Meller, *Peter Vischer d. Ä. und seine Werkstatt*, 1925, p. 190; E. Panofsky, *Hercules am Scheideweg und andere antike Bildstoffe in der neueren Kunst* (*Studien d. Bibliothek Warburg* 18); D. Wuttke, *Die "Histori Herculis" des Nürnberger Humanisten und Freundes der Gebrüder Vischer, Pangratz Bernhaubt gen. Schwenter* (Diss., Tübingen), 1956; H. Stafski, *Der jüngere Peter Vischer*, 1962, pp. 50, 68 ff.; D. Wuttke, "The *Histori Herculis* by the Nuremberg Humanist and Friend of the Vischer Brothers, Pangratz Bernhaubt, called Schwenter," *Beihefte zum Archiv für Kulturgeschichte*, vol. 7, 1964, pp. 112 ff.

The two drawings (cat. 57 and 58) are illustrations for the *Histori Herculis* by Pankratz Bernhaupt, called Schwenter. Their source is a manuscript of 1515, now in the city library of Nuremberg. Pankratz Bernhaupt, who was attached to the City Council of Nuremberg in a capacity similar to that of Master of Ceremonies, received a humanistic education and was a friend of the brothers Hermann and Peter Vischer the Younger, sharing with the latter a common interest in classical literature.

The *Histori Herculis* was the German translation of a Latin humanist drama, composed by an unidentified "poeta laureatus" of Rhenish origin in the circle of Sebastian Brant. The work retells the legend, recorded by Xenophon, of Hercules at the crossroads. The original decision the young hero had to make regarding the road designating his life is here modified into a choice between vice and virtue imposed upon the matured hero. In his play Schwenter utilized parts of a Latin translation by Jakob Locher of the *Ship of Fools* by Sebastian Brant.

The literary context explains also the iconographic dependence of the drawings by Vischer the Younger upon the woodcuts in the Latin edition of the *Ship of Fools*, published in Strasburg in 1497. As Panofsky has shown the *Dream of Hercules* is depicted according to the iconographic formula of the *Judgment of Paris*. The identical representation of the two legends, whose common moralizing character was already recognized in late antiquity, is found for the first time in the above-mentioned edition of the *Ship of Fools*. In Vischer's drawing a figure identified as the God of Sleep by the inscription *Somnus* lightly touches Hercules with a wand. Somnus wears the petasus and sandals of Mercury, and these attributes prove that the iconography was based upon scenes from the *Judgment of Paris*. The Fates —also designated by inscriptions—replace the three goddesses. Lachesis and Clotho are inspired by similar figures in Dürer's engravings; Atropos, who stands in the center, is derived, according to Panofsky, from the standing Leda of Leonardo da Vinci. The Fates should be interpreted here as the antique heralds of Memento Mori, who underline the moralizing intention of the composition.

Still more than the *Dream of Hercules* the drawing *Virtutes et Voluptas* relates to the illustrations in the Latin edition of the *Ship of Fools*. Voluptas, her companions, and the fountain were all conceived following the example of the corresponding woodcut. The jaws of Hell—Orcus with the three-headed Cerberus—is a warning of the consequences awaiting those who abandon themselves to Voluptas. In the background Virtutes (in the text this allegorical female figure is also designated by the plural) climbs a steep and rocky path. The female figure with the distaff is no longer related to the Virtue of antiquity but is portrayed in the text as old and hideous. The person kneeling at the left in the middle ground before the fire, and who bears the inscription Odium, is Envy spying on the virtuous. Thus the second page represents the actual content of the dream which Somnus sends to Hercules.

MATHIS GOTHART NITHART (GRÜNEWALD)

Painter and designer of fountains. Probably born around 1475-80 in Würzburg. Lived from 1501 to 1525 in Seligenstadt-on-Main; court painter to Archbishop Uriel von Gemmingen, Prince Elector of Mainz, from 1508 to about 1512; worked around the years 1512-15 in the Antonite Cloister of Isenheim in Alsace; from 1516 to 1526 court painter to Cardinal Albrecht of Brandenburg, Elector of Mainz; lived in Frankfurt in 1526-27 at the house of the silk embroiderer Hans von Saarbrücken; died before September 1, 1528, in Halle-on-Saale.

BIBLIOGRAPHY: H. A. Schmid, *Die Gemälde und Zeichnungen von Matthias Grünewald*, 1908-11; O. Hagen, *Matthias Grünewald*, 1919; W. F. Storck, *Handzeichnungen Grünewalds* (1st ed. of the "*Gesellschaft f. zeichnende Künste*"), 1922; M. J. Friedländer, *Die Grünewaldzeichnungen der Sammlung Savigny*, 1926; Id., *Die Zeichnungen von Matthias Grünewald*, 1927; H. Feurstein, *Matthias Grünewald*, 1930; R. Graul, *Grünewalds Zeichnungen*, 1935; W. Fraenger, *Matthias Grünewald. Ein physiognomischer Versuch*, 1936; W. K. Zülch, *Der historische Grünewald, Mathis Gothart Nithart*, 1938; G. Schönberger, *The Drawings of Mathis Gothart Nithart, called Grünewald*, 1948; F. Winkler in

B.M., n.s. 2, 1952, pp. 32 ff.; L. Behling, *Die Zeichnungen des Mathis Gothart Nithart genannt Grünewald*, 1955; N. Pevsner-M. Meier, *Grünewald* (in English), 1958; A. Weixlgärtner, *Grünewald*, 1962.

59. *Kneeling Figure with Two Angels*

Chalk, heightened with white on heavily toned paper. 286 x 366 mm, 11¼ x 14⅜ in.

Coll. Radowitz. Acquired 1856. KdZ 2040.

BIBLIOGRAPHY: Schmid, p. 258; Lippmann-Grote, 2nd ed., no. 180; O. Hagen in *Kunstchronik*, n.s. 28, 1916-17, pp. 73 ff.; Id., *Grünewald*, pp. 186-88; L. Réau, *Matthias Grünewald et le Retable de Colmar*, 1920, p. 293; Friedländer-Bock, p. 44; Storck, pl. 17; R. Weser in *Archiv f. christl. Kunst* 40, 1926, p. 7; Behling, no. 23; Friedländer, 1927, p. 24; Feurstein, p. 141; H. Kehrer in *Forschungen zur Kirchengeschichte*, 1932, p. 211; F. Winkler, *Mittelniederrheinische und west-fälische Handzeichnungen des 15. und 16. Jahrhunderts* (*Die Meisterzeichnung* 4), 1932, no. 50; Graul, nos. 18-19; Fraenger, pp. 147 ff.; A. Burkhard, *Matthias Grünewald. Personality and Accomplishment*, 1936, p. 71; Zülch, p. 355; Id., *Grünewald, Mathis Neithart, genannt Gothart*, 1954, pl. 25; Winkler, *Altdeutsche Zeichnungen*, p. 61; Schönberger, no. 17; E. Poeschel in *ZKG* 13, 1950, pp. 92 ff.; Pevsner-Meier, no. 25; *Deutsche Zeichnungen 1400-1900*, no. 72; Weixlgärtner, p. 116.

The scene represented in this drawing has been given diverse interpretations. The Berlin catalogue views the principal figure as an angel of the Annunciation. Schmid, Feurstein, Zülch, Winkler, Schönberger, and Halm see in the figure the Christ of a Coronation of the Virgin. Hagen, Fraenger, and Weser read the figure as one of the three kings in an Adoration of the Magi. Weixlgärtner, agreeing with a suggestion by Panofsky, thinks it likely that the subject is the rarely depicted scene of the Decree of the Redemption. Those who interpret the scene as a study for a Coronation of the Virgin establish a relationship between the drawing and the commission given in 1514 by Canon Heinrich Reitzmann for a painting of the Gloriosissima Virgo. None of the present interpretations seems entirely convincing: The Coronation of the Virgin and the Decree of the Redemption are scenes which generally take place above the clouds, in heaven, so that the tree which appears in the drawing contradicts these interpretations. Moreover Mathis Nithart, as is shown in the Berlin studies for the *Madonna of Stuppach* and for the *Annunciation* of the Isenheim Altar (cat. 60), placed his figures from the very first within the context of the definitive composition. On the other hand the angels, as well as the crown, scepter, and astrolabe, could only belong to a member of the Trinity. The absence of a beard and the crown resting lightly on the forehead make it unlikely that the figure in question is Christ. Though the iconographic problem remains unsolved, this page is one of the most important examples of the artist's mastery of draftsmanship. On the verso (not illustrated) is a chalk sketch, considerably faded, of the Virgin with the Infant Christ and St. John, recalling an Italian composition of the High Renaissance.

60. *Kneeling Virgin, for an Annunciation*

Chalk on darkened paper. 160 x 146 mm, 6¼ x 5¾ in.

Coll. Savigny. Acquired 1925. KdZ 12 037.

BIBLIOGRAPHY: Friedländer, *Slg. Savigny*, no. 1; Id., *Grünewald-Zeichnungen*, pl. 14; Graul, no. 6; Fraenger, p. 93; Burkhard, p. 69; Feurstein, p. 140; Behling, no. 19; Winkler in *B.M.*, n.s. 2, 1952, pp. 32 ff.; Pevsner-Meier, no. 21; Weixlgärtner, pp. 112 ff., no. 12.

This drawing is a study for the *Annunciation* of the Isenheim altarpiece. A second study, differing from this in the placement of the head, hands, and folds of the cloak, is also in Berlin (KdZ 12 040). We share Winkler's opinion that the study shown here is the later one, as the Virgin's position is much closer to the painting. The drawing was probably executed around 1512, at the time when Grünewald was at work on the Isenheim altarpiece.

61. Recto: *Head of a Singing Angel*

Chalk. Watermark: tall crown with cross and star. 276 x 196 mm, 10⅞ x 7¾ in. The monogram, at the lower right, was added later.

Coll. v. Nagler (Lugt 2529). Acquired 1835. KdZ 1070.

62. Verso: *Study for the Head of a Young Woman*

BIBLIOGRAPHY: Lippmann-Grote, 2nd ed., no. 182 (angel); Schmid, p. 260; Friedländer-Bock, p. 44; Hagen, p. 194; Réau, p. 293; Friedländer, *Grünewald-Zeichnungen*, pl. 30; Feurstein, p. 143; Graul, nos. 11 and 23; Fraenger, p. 336; Schönberger, nos. 23 and 24; Behling, nos. 31 and 32; *Deutsche Zeichnungen 1400-1900*, no. 73 (angel); Pevsner-Meier, no. 29; Weixlgärtner, p. 118.

The head on the recto has been interpreted to be that of a singing or wailing angel, and is closely linked to another Berlin drawing of a weeping angel (KdZ 12 319). The iconographic context to which the two drawings belong has also been given diverse interpretations. Zülch thinks it is a study for a work once in the Cathedral of Mainz but stolen by the Swedes about 1631-32 during the Thirty Years' War.

According to a description of the work given by Sandrart in the *Teutsche Academie der Bau- Bild- und Mahlerey-Künste* (1675), this panel depicted a blind hermit who while crossing the frozen Rhine, accompanied by a small boy, was attacked by two bandits. A copy of the painting still existed at the beginning of the nineteenth century in a Frankfurt private collection. Pevsner and Meier have recently come to agree with Zülch's point of view. Feurstein, Winkler, and Schönberger are of the opinion that these two pages are studies for angels that must have been part of a Lamentation of Christ or a Martyrdom of St. Sebastian, in the style of those found in the woodcut by Baldung Grien (B.37). This study is generally dated 1520. Only Schönberger places it around 1515-16, because of the stylistic analogy with the angel in the *Angel Choir* of the Isenheim altarpiece. The angel in the foreground of the *Angel Choir* illustrates this relationship, while the angels in the St. Sebastian panel of the same altarpiece are of an altogether different type. Although the hypothesis of the hermit accompanied by the weeping boy is a tempting one, no supporting proof exists.

There also is no agreement concerning the interpretation of the head on the verso of the drawing. Certain scholars consider it to represent a man, others a woman. The hair style, however, would seem to indicate a female figure. Zülch views it as a study for a female saint that would have figured in the other Mainz altarpiece carried off by the Swedes. Schönberger reads it as a Virgin. There is a decided relationship to the Virgin and Child of the Isenheim altarpiece. Following Schönberger it seems logical to date both studies at the same period as the Isenheim altarpiece, although perhaps one or two years later than 1515-16.

LUCAS CRANACH THE ELDER

Painter, engraver, and designer of woodcuts. Born in Kronach (Franconia) in 1472. Active from 1504 in Wittenberg. Died in Weimar in 1553.

BIBLIOGRAPHY: Th.L. Girshausen, *Die Handzeichnungen Lucas Cranachs d.Ä.* (Diss. Frankfurt), 1936; Cranach-Ausstellung, *Lucas Cranach d.Ä. und Lucas Cranach d.J. Gemälde, Zeichnungen, Graphik*. Berlin, 1937; J. Rosenberg, *Die Zeichnungen Lucas Cranachs d.Ä.*, 1960.

63. *A Thief on the Cross (turned toward the right)*

Black chalk, heightened with white on reddish tinted paper. Watermark: crown (not mentioned in Briquet). 226 x 121 mm, 8⅞ x 4¾ in.

Coll. F. Bamberger and v. Lanna. Acquired 1910. KdZ 4450.

64. *A Thief on the Cross (turned toward the left)*

Charcoal, heightened with white on reddish tinted paper. Watermark: see cat. 63. 215 x 128 mm, 8½ x 5 in.

Provenance: see cat. 63. KdZ 4451.

BIBLIOGRAPHY: Schönbrunner-Meder, no. 1097; M. J. Friedländer in *RKW* 31, 1908, p. 394; J. Bets in *MKW* 4, 1911, p. 25; Friedländer-Bock, p. 19; C. Glaser, *Lucas Cranach*, 1921, pp. 18 and 200; Id., *Lucas Cranachs d. Ä. Handzeichnungen*, 2nd ed. of *Ges. f. Zeichn. Künste*, 1922, pl. I-II; M. J. Friedländer-J. Rosenberg, *Die Gemälde von Lucas Cranach*, 1932, p. 3, nos. 11-12; Girshausen, nos. 1-2; *Cranach-Ausstellung*, nos. 154-155; F. Thöne, *Lucas Cranach d.Ä. Meisterzeichnungen*, 1939, p. 8; Winkler, *Altdeutsche Zeichnungen*, pp. 73 ff.; Id., *Die grossen Zeichner*, 1951, p. 48; *Meisterwerke aus den Berliner Museen. Deutsche Zeichnungen d. Dürerzeit*. Berlin Exhibition 1952, no. 229 a-b; Rosenberg, nos. 2-3.

These drawings (see also cat. 64) were originally attributed to Grünewald. V. Meder subsequently published them as the work of an anonymous artist of the end of the fifteenth century. It was Friedländer who recognized the drawings as youthful works by Cranach, probably done around 1502 during his stay in Vienna. The close relationship between these two drawings and the engraved and painted Crucifixions of Cranach's youth leaves no doubt that Friedländer's attribution is the correct one. The strongly expressive quality of Cranach's drawing at this period, which also marks his first woodcuts, seems to have had a decisive influence on the stylistic formation of the Danube School. Altdorfer's drawing *Landscape with a Pair of Lovers* (cat. 126) clearly shows the extent to which Cranach's art influenced the younger artists of his time.

65. *Lucretia*

Pen and brown ink. 131 x 95 mm, 5⅛ x 3¾ in. Signed with Cranach's winged serpent and the date 1509.

Coll. King Friedrich-Wilhelm I (Lugt 1631). KdZ 504.

BIBLIOGRAPHY: Lippmann-Grote, 2nd ed., no. 201; Friedländer-Bock, p. 19; C. Glaser, *Lucas Cranachs d.Ä. Handzeichnungen*, pp. 13, 15, pl. VI; Friedländer-Rosenberg, no. 198 e (mentioned); Girshausen, no. 19; Rosenberg, no. 16.

The suicide of Lucretia, as an example of womanly virtue, was one of the most popular antique themes at this time. Moreover, it offered the artist one of the rare occasions to portray a female nude. This work is the only drawing by Cranach which bears as a signature the winged serpent from the coat of arms that had been granted him in 1508. Cranach painted the suicide of Lucretia several times, but only the painting in Coburg (Friedländer-Rosenberg no. 102) is closely related to this drawing.

66. *Boar and Dogs*

Pen and brown ink. Watermark: tall crown (variant of Briquet 4971 and 4988). 150 x 241 mm, 5⅞ x 9½ in. At the lower edge Dürer's monogram has been forged and then erased.

Coll. Neville D. Goldsmid (Lugt 1962) and Suermondt (Lugt 415). Acquired 1879. KdZ 386.

BIBLIOGRAPHY: F. Lippmann, *Lucas Cranach*, 1895, p. 7; Lippmann-Grote, 2nd ed., no. 202; Friedländer-Bock, p. 20; Girshausen, no. 66; *Cranach-Ausstellung*, no. 198; Thöne, pp. 16 ff.; Rosenberg, no. 60.

Like Dürer, Cranach was an excellent draftsman of animals, much praised by his contemporaries for his naturalistic depictions of stags, boars, and other game. Christoph Scheurl, in a dedicatory letter in Latin addressed to the artist, tells us that Cranach made sketches of animals during the royal hunts. The princes are said to have derived as much pleasure from these drawings as from the hunt itself.

The drawing shown here should be considered in relation to the woodcut *Stag Hunt* (ca. 1506) and other later hunting scenes. Nonetheless Rosenberg dated this page in the vicinity of 1510-20. It is difficult to determine whether this study actually belonged to those made during a hunt. A comparison of the drawing style seen here—rapid but astonishingly sure—to that of the finished drawing of the boars (with watercolor added) in Dresden (Rosenberg nos. 64-66) lends support to the opinion that the Berlin drawing is an actual study after nature. The Louvre has a study of stags which is very close to the Berlin drawing.

67. *Portrait of a Beardless Man*

Brush and oil paint on brownish tinted paper. Torn paper, a piece added below, and mounted on canvas. 223 x 160 mm, 8¾ x 6¼ in.

Transferred from the Gemäldegalerie to the Print Room in 1910. KdZ 4478.

BIBLIOGRAPHY: Friedländer-Bock, p. 20; Friedländer-Rosenberg, no. 56 (mentioned); *Propyläenkunstgeschichte*, vol. 10, p. 20; J. Rosenberg in *JPKS* 55, 1934, p. 181; Girshausen, no. 42; *Cranach-Ausstellung*, no. 204; Thöne, p. 18; Winkler, *Altdeutsche Zeichnungen*, p. 74; Id., *Die Grossen Zeichner*, 1951, pp. 48 and 51; *Deutsche Zeichnungen 1400-1900*, no. 50; J. Rosenberg, *A Loan Exhibition of Fifteen Portrait Drawings of Reims*. Cleveland, Ohio, 1952; Rosenberg, no. 73.

Although this oil on paper is not strictly speaking a drawing, specialists have always considered it as such. As the famous portrait drawings in Reims reveal, the artist seems to have used oil freely in his preparatory studies for portraits. The close relationship of this work to the portrait of a Burgomaster of Weissenfels (Saxony) dates it around 1515-20.

68. *Project for a Polyptych with a Lamentation of Christ*

Pen with brown and black ink, heightened with watercolor. 393 x 247 mm, 15½ x 9¾ in. Inscribed with a serpent in the lower right corner of the central panel; below, Lucas Cranach is inscribed by an unknown hand. The upper part of the central panel was drawn on a separate sheet which was then pasted to this one.

Coll. v. Rumohr (Lugt 2160). KdZ 387.

BIBLIOGRAPHY: C. Schuchardt, *Lucas Cranach d.Ä. Leben und Werk*, 1851-71, 2nd part, p. 26, no. 40; Lippmann-Grote, 2nd ed., no. 203; Friedländer-Bock, p. 19; Girshausen, no. 35; *Cranach-Ausstellung*, no. 158; Rosenberg, no. 31.

A typical model drawing of German Renaissance altarpieces, this page was presented to the donor for approval before the painter proceeded to execute the commission.

This particular project was to have two pairs of movable wings, each depicting the figure of a saint. For the exterior of the stationary panels of the closed altar the artist planned two isolated figures. The Berlin model is incomplete, but we are able partially to complete it, thanks to copies in Erlangen (E. Bock, *Die Zeichnungen in der Universitätsbibliothek Erlangen*, 1929, nos. 1274, 1279-1282). The saints portrayed are identified in notes written by the artist.

According to these inscriptions the altarpiece was to depict the following saints:

A. Outer wings when closed

——— St. Titus ——— [St. Paul]

B. With inner panels closed

St. Mark   St. Andrew   St. Timothy   [St. Luke]

C. Central panel when open

St. Peter   The Lamentation   St. Barnabas

The predella was never executed. A possible date for the model drawing is 1518-20.

LUCAS CRANACH THE YOUNGER

Painter and designer of woodcuts. Born October 4, 1515, in Wittenberg. Trained by his father. Died January 25, 1586, in Weimar.

69. *Portrait of a Man with a Beard*

Brush, heightened with watercolor and gouache on yellowish-brown tinted paper. 253 x 177 mm, 10 x 7 in.

Coll. Le Roye-Ladurie and Suermondt (Lugt 415). Acquired 1874. KdZ 2378.

BIBLIOGRAPHY: A. Woltmann, *Hans Holbein und seine Zeit*, 2nd ed., vol. 2, p. 119; Lippmann-Grote, 1st ed., no. 13; Friedländer-Bock, p. 20; Friedländer-Bock, *Handzeichnungen*, pl. 55; O. Götz, *Altdeutsche Porträtzeichnungen*, pl. 4; Girshausen, no. 85; *Cranach-Ausstellung*, no. 208; E. H. Zimmermann in *B M* 63, 1942, pp. 1 ff.; Rosenberg, no. 92.

In the literature this drawing is alternately attributed to Cranach the Younger and the Elder. Technically it does not differ from the portrait drawings of the later period of Cranach the Elder. The pinkish skin tone and the conscious absence of any relief in the face are, nonetheless, already characteristic of the younger Cranach's style. Rosenberg attributes the work to Cranach the Elder, giving the date in the vicinity of 1540-45. Its great similarity to the *Portrait of Duke Augustus of Saxony*, unquestionably by Cranach the Younger (Friedländer-Rosenberg, no. 345), makes us prone to favor an attribution to the latter artist.

HANS SÜSS VON KULMBACH

Painter, designer of woodcuts and windows. Born around 1480, probably in Kulmbach (Franconia). Worked in Dürer's studio from about 1500 and also may have worked for a time with Jacopo de' Barbari. Acquired rights of citizenship in Nuremberg in 1511. Received commission in Cracow in 1514-16. Died between November 29 and December 3, 1522.

BIBLIOGRAPHY: Friedrich Winkler, *Die Zeichnungen Hans Süss von Kulmbachs und Hans Leonhard Schäufeleins*, 1942; Id., *Hans von Kulmbach. Leben und Werk eines fränkischen Künstlers der Dürerzeit*, 1959.

70. *Three Studies of Women's Costumes*

Pen and brown ink upon preparatory drawing in pencil. Watermark: hand (variant of Briquet 11 424). 183 x 202 mm, 7¼ x 8 in. Scrawled Dürer monogram added later.

Coll. v. Beckerath (Lugt 2504). Acquired 1902. KdZ 5467.

BIBLIOGRAPHY: Lippmann-Grote, 2nd ed., no. 220; F. Winkler in *OMD* 10, 1936, p. 68; Id., *Kulmbach-Schäufelein-Zeichnungen*, nos. 8-9; Id., *Altdeutsche Zeichnungen*, pp. 39 ff.; Id., *Kulmbach*, pp. 13, 14, 21; L. Oehler, in *MJKW* 17, 1959, p. 144; *Meister um Dürer*, no. 197.

Winkler was the first to see in this drawing—always believed to be Netherlandish (Lippmann-Grote, ibid.)—a very early work by Kulmbach. The former error in attribution is easily explicable, however, by the costumes which, as the catalogue of the Nuremberg exhibition has also shown, are Netherlandish or at least Westphalian. Strangely enough the watermark would indicate a similar provenance: northern France. On the other hand, the composition and hastily scrawled Dürer monogram on the verso clearly show the drawing to be a product of the Dürer circle. In any case there has been no evidence of any visit by Kulmbach to the Netherlands, nor do there exist any other allusions in his work that would indicate a more profound knowledge of the Netherlands and its art.

71. *Half-Length Portrait of Abbot Johannes Rottenecker of the Monastery of St. Egidius of Nuremberg*

Pen and brown ink. 175 x 204 mm, 6⅞ x 8 in.

Coll. Triqueti (Lugt 1304), Rogers (Lugt 625), and Posonyi-Hulot. Acquired 1877. KdZ 48.

BIBLIOGRAPHY: K. Koelitz, *Hans Süss von Kulmbach und seine Werke* (Diss., Zurich), 1891, p. 77; W. v. Seydlitz in *Beilage zur Allgemeinen Zeitung*, 1894, no. 58; *Literarische Rundschau* 1894, p. 166; F. Wickhoff in *ZBK*, n.s. 17, 1906, p. 217; S. Stiassny in *Kunstchronik* 22, 1886-87, p. 503; G. v. Térey, *Die Handzeichnungen des Hans Baldung gen. Grien*, vol. 1, 1894, p. 37; H. Schmitz, *Die Glasgemälde des Königl. Kunstgewerbemuseums in Berlin*, vol. 1, 1913, pp. 158-59; M. Weinberger, *Nürnberger Malerei an der Wende zur Renaissance und die Anfänge der Dürerschule (Studien z. dt. Kunstgeschichte, 217)*, 1921, p. 189; Friedländer-Bock, p. 60; H. Bermann, *Hans Süss von Kulmbach* (Diss., Leipzig), 1923, p. 28; K. T. Parker, *Drawings of the Early German Schools*, 1926, no. 23; H. Röttinger in *MJBK*, n.s. 4, 1927, pp. 17 ff.; E. Bock, *Die Zeichnungen in der Universitätsbibliothek Erlangen*, 1929, no. 234; F. Winkler in *JPKS*, 50, 1929, pp. 11 ff.; F. Stadler, *Hans von Kulmbach*, 1936, p. 29 and no. 50 a-c; Winkler,

Kulmbach-Schäufelein-Zeichnungen, nos. 131-33 (132); Id., *Kulmbach*, pp. 13, 76; *Meister um Albrecht Dürer*, no. 212.

A drawing in Strasburg and one in Erlangen also portray abbots of St. Egidius, Nuremberg. Kulmbach made six of these studies for windows. Two of these windows, formerly in the Kunstgewerbe Museum in Berlin (destroyed during the war), and a window in Nuremberg were numbered 1, 5, and 6; according to Parker there is a fourth window in an English private collection. The Nuremberg window is dated 1511. As opposed to the small drawing for the window known as the *Emperor's Window* (cat. 72) these are more finished drawings for the use of the glass painter.

72. *Design for a Window*

Pen and brown ink, lightly heightened with watercolor. 225 x 126 mm, 8⅞ x 5 in.

Part of the original collection. KdZ 4278.

BIBLIOGRAPHY: E. Bock in *MKW* 11, 1909, pp. 401 ff.; H. Schinnerer in *Die christliche Kunst* 6, 1909-10, pp. 328 ff.; H. Schmitz, *Die Glasgemälde d. Königl. Kunstgewerbemuseums zu Berlin*, 2nd vol., 1913, p. 172; Friedländer-Bock, p. 60; Winkler, *Kulmbach-Schäufelein-Zeichnungen*, no. 79; Id., *Kulmbach*, p. 76.

This work, along with three other drawings, is part of a series of projects drawn by Kulmbach for the window known as the *Emperor's Window* in the choir of St. Sebaldus in Nuremberg. It was to replace an older damaged work. Letters from the Emperor Maximilian survive which concern the replacement of the old window. In a letter of February 5, 1514, the Emperor asked the Council of Nuremberg to appoint one of their members, Melchior Pfinzing, to see that the project was executed. In two subsequent letters the price of 200 florins was agreed upon, thus Kulmbach's designs must date from this same year. The four sections shown here formed the lower left quarter of the window, representing as follows:

Above left: Figure in Near Eastern dress with the coat of arms of Granada
     right: St. Elizabeth of Thuringia
Below left: Soldier with the coat of arms of Slavonia
     right: Lansquenet with the arms of Alsace

73. *The Annunciation*

Charcoal. 389 x 299 mm, 15¼ x 11¾ in. Damaged in the lower left. Date 1512.

Part of the original collection. KdZ 3135.

BIBLIOGRAPHY: Rieffel in *ZCHK* 10, 1897, p. 129 (Grünewald); Lippmann-Grote, 2nd ed., no. 152; H. A. Schmid, *Matthias Grünewald*, 1911, p. 21, 284; Friedländer-Bock, pp. 59 ff.; Friedländer-Bock, *Handzeichnungen*, pl. 45; Winkler in *JPKS* 50, 1929, p. 35; F. Stadler, *Hans von Kulmbach*, 1936, p. 27 and no. 67; Winkler, *Kulmbach-Schäufelein-Zeichnungen*, no. 44; Id., *Kulmbach*, p. 79; *Meister um Albrecht Dürer*, no. 208.

As opposed to Stadler, who considers it a study for a painting, Winkler believes this outstanding page by Kulmbach to be a sketch for a window. The catalogue of the exhibition Masters of the Dürer Circle affirms Winkler's thesis. Kulmbach's other works offer no points of comparison that would allow us to determine precisely whether the work in question is a preparatory drawing for a painting or for a window.

HANS SCHÄUFELEIN

Painter and designer of woodcuts and painted glass. Probably born around 1480-85. Worked in Dürer's studio between 1503-04 and 1506-07, then in Augsburg with Hans Holbein the Elder. Around 1509-10 he was in the Tyrol and from 1510 to 1515 once again moved to Augsburg. He settled in Nördlingen in 1515, where he died in the autumn of 1540.

BIBLIOGRAPHY: H. Wallach, *Die Stilentwicklung Hans Leonhard Schäufeleins*, 1st part (Diss. Munich, 1926), 1929; F. Winkler, *Die Zeichnungen Hans Süss von Kulmbachs und Hans Leonhard Schäufeleins*, 1942; *Zeichnungen*.

74. *The Nativity*

Pen and black ink. Watermark: ox head (Briquet 15 256). 278 x 188 mm, 10⅞ x 7⅜ in. At the bottom Dürer's monogram and the date 1507 added later by an unknown hand.

From a Danish private collection. Acquired 1924. KdZ 11 963.

BIBLIOGRAPHY: E. Buchner, "Der junge Schäufelein als Maler und Zeichner" in *Festschrift für M. J. Friedländer zum 60. Geburtstage*, 1927, p. 60; H. Tietze, "Aus der Werkstatt Dürers" in ibid., pp. 44 ff.; Wallach, 1st part, p. 24; Winkler, *Kulmbach-Schäufelein-Zeichnungen*, no. 10; Id., *Altdeutsche Zeichnungen*, pp. 40 ff.; *Meister um Albrecht Dürer*, no. 308.

Here Schäufelein's composition is very close to the one used by Dürer for the altarpiece known as the Baumgartner Altar, as well as for the engravings *Christmas* (B.2) and the *Nativity* from the series *The Life of the Virgin* (B.85) by the same artist. The date 1507 inscribed at the same time as the counterfeit Dürer monogram accords perfectly with the style.

75. *Lady Wearing a Headdress*

Pen and black ink. 278 x 193 mm, 10⅞ x 7⅝ in. Signed with monogram and a shovel.

Coll. v. Lanna. Acquired 1910. KdZ 4462.

BIBLIOGRAPHY: Schönbrunner-Meder, no. 1302; Friedländer-Bock, p. 76; Wallach, p. 28; Winkler, *Kulmbach-Schäufelein-Zeichnungen*, no. 23; *Meister um Albrecht Dürer*, no. 309.

This drawing exemplifies Schäufelein's style in the years 1507-09. During this period, in which he was strongly influenced by Dürer, the artist produced his most harmonious drawings.

76. *Portrait of a Man*

Black chalk. 285 x 216 mm, 11¼ x 8½ in. Watermark: ox head with crown and flower (Briquet 15 221). Inscribed with monogram and shovel and dated 1520.

Coll. King Friedrich-Wilhelm I. KdZ 1295.

BIBLIOGRAPHY: Lippmann-Grote, 2nd ed., no. 153; Friedländer-Bock, pp. 75 ff.; Friedländer-Bock, *Handzeichnungen*, pl. 43; E. Buchner in Thieme-Becker XXIX, p. 557; Winkler, *Kulmbach-Schäufelein-Zeichnungen*, no. 70.

It is uncertain whether this page is a character study or the portrait of a specific sitter. One of the best surviving portraits from the Dürer circle, the Berlin drawing is closely related to four character studies in the Kunsthistoriches Museum, Vienna, and in the Kister collection, Kreuzlingen, Switzerland (see *Meister um Albrecht Dürer*, no. 299 a-d, figs. 60-61). The *Head of a Man with a Beard* in the Kister collection (no. 299 d, fig. 61) is especially close to the Berlin work. (The portraits in the Kister collection are dated 1511.) As opposed to the linear style characteristic of the Dürer circle, the Berlin drawing is rendered in a very soft and pictorial manner. The artist used the stump of the chalk extensively, particularly in the treatment of the face and beard.

BARTHEL BEHAM

Born in Nuremberg, probably in 1502. Banished from that city with his brother Sebald and Jörg Penz for expressing anarchistic and atheistic ideas. Worked from about 1527 for the Dukes of Bavaria. Died probably in 1540 while traveling in Italy.

77. *Moses Rescued from the Bulrushes*

> Pen and watercolor. Watermark: small crown (see Briquet 4805). 156 x 175 mm, 6⅛ x 6⅞ in.
>
> Coll. King Friedrich-Wilhelm I. KdZ 1062.
>
> BIBLIOGRAPHY: G. Pauli in Thieme-Becker, III, p. 192; Lippmann-Grote, 2nd ed., no. 156; Friedländer-Bock, p. 12; *Meister um Albrecht Dürer*, no. 39.

This drawing dates from perhaps the late 1520's. From a stylistic standpoint it is close to the engravings *Madonna before a Curtain* (Pauli 7) and *Madonna at a Window* (Pauli 9).

HANS SEBALD BEHAM

Miniaturist, engraver, etcher, and designer of woodcuts and windows. Born in Nuremberg in 1500. Banished from that city in 1525 for anarchist and atheistic opinions, he nonetheless returned the same year. He fled again in 1528 after publishing, against the Council's orders, a book on equine proportions. He is supposed to have plagiarized a part of this manuscript from Dürer. Active in Munich in 1530, then entered the service of Cardinal Albrecht of Brandenburg. Settled in Frankfurt-on-Main in 1532, where he died on November 22, 1550.

78. *The Massacre of the Innocents*

> Pen and brown ink with pale gray wash, and pale pink flesh tones in watercolor. 230 mm diam., 9 in. Date 1522 added later.
>
> Coll. Oppenheimer (Lugt 1351). Given in 1932. KdZ 15 098.
>
> BIBLIOGRAPHY: K. T. Parker, *Drawings of the Early German Schools*, 1926, no. 29; *BM* 54, 1933, p. 44; *Meister um Albrecht Dürer*, no. 85.

This drawing is part of a series divided among Berlin, Frankfurt-on-Main, Oxford, and London (British Museum), which depicts, for the most part, scenes from the Passion. The others are generally inferior in quality to the *Massacre of the Innocents*. The red lines were probably placed there by the glass designer to indicate the sections of glass to be cut, as well as the placement of the lead. The letters "r" and "p" are color indications. Although inscribed by another hand, the date 1522 would seem to be correct.

LEONHARD BECK

Painter, designer of woodcuts. Born around 1480 in Augsburg. Traveled with Hans Holbein the Elder to Frankfurt in 1501. Master artist in Augsburg from 1503 until his death in 1542.

79. *Portrait of Count Moritz von Ertingen*

Black, red, and yellow chalk with wash. 345 x 275 mm, 13½ x 10¾ in.

Coll. Guichardot and Suermondt (Lugt 415). Acquired 1879. KdZ 523.

BIBLIOGRAPHY: Lippmann-Grote, 1st ed., no. 79; G. Pauli in Thieme-Becker III, p. 192; Friedländer-Bock, p. 12; F. Winkler, *Augsburger Malerbildnisse*, 1948, pp. 23 ff.

The sitter is identified in a subsequent notation on the verso of this page: "Graff Moritz von Ertinger" (more correctly, Ertingen), "1521." This sheet, as well as its pendant, are hardly mentioned in the literature, in spite of the rarity of colored chalk drawings in German art. Winkler attributes to Leonhard Beck the two drawings listed in the Berlin catalogue as works of Barthel Beham. In any case they belong to the School of Augsburg and not to that of Nuremberg.

PETER FLÖTNER

Wood sculptor, cabinetmaker, goldsmith, and engraver on wood. Born around 1485, died in Nuremberg in 1546.

80. *Design for a Ceremonial Chair*

Pen and brown ink, heightened with brown and black watercolor. 186 x 156 mm, 7¼ x 6⅛ in. Signed at the lower left: P. Flo[e]. Upper corners cut.

Coll. v. Nagler (Lugt 2529). Acquired 1835. KdZ 390.

BIBLIOGRAPHY: G. K. Nagler, *Die Monogrammisten*, vol. 4, 1871, p. 874; A. v. Hefner-Alteneck, *Trachten und Kunstwerke*, vol. 1, 1852, pl. 65, vol. 7, 1886, p. 477; A. Lichtwarck, *Der Ornamentstich*, 1888, p. 146; Reimers, *Peter Flötner nach seinen Handzeichnungen und Holzschnitten*, 1890, p. 4, 101; Lange, *Peter Flötner*, 1897, p. 50; Haupt in *JPKS* 26, 1905, p. 154; Friedländer-Bock, p. 42; E. F. Bange in *JPKS* 57, 1936, no. 6.

On several occasions Flötner made drawings and woodcuts of designs for furniture and other utensils, as well as two designs for organs (Berlin). When designing this armchair he seems to have attached greater significance to the richness and diversity of decoration than to the practicality of the chair. The seat seems out of proportion, largely due to the abnormal height of the back. A variant or copy of this work is found in Basel. The close relation between the style of the chair and that of the two organs, dated 1527, leads us to place this drawing in the vicinity of 1527-28.

81. *Design for a Dagger*

Pen and black ink with yellowish-brown wash. 422 x 121 mm, 16⅝ x 4¾ in. Cut and pasted on brown-toned paper. Dated 1539.

Coll. Thomas Thane (Lugt 1544). Acquired 1938. KdZ 16 779.

BIBLIOGRAPHY: F. Bange in *JPKS* 59, 1938, pp. 231 ff.; Winkler, *Altdeutsche Zeichnungen*, p. 43.

This drawing was attributed to Flötner by Bange. Among other designs by this artist we also find models for metalwork, sword handles, etc. Here the artist has drawn the handle and sheath of a dagger, following the style popular in Germany during the third decade of the sixteenth century. The end of the sheath is missing. Bange concludes that this drawing was destined for publication as a woodcut.

AUGUSTIN HIRSCHVOGEL

Painter, engraver, and engineer. Born in Nuremberg in 1503 and died in 1553 in Vienna.

82. *The Castle of Neuburg on the Danube*

Pen and brown ink on paper tinted white over a sketch in silverpoint. 181 x 307 mm, 7⅛ x 12⅛ in. Acquired 1913. KdZ 4714.

BIBLIOGRAPHY: K. Schwarz, *Augustin Hirschvogel*, 1917, pp. 122, 206; Fried-länder-Bock, p. 45; A. Schmitt in *B.M.*, n.s. 4, 1954, pp. 8 ff.; Id., *Hanns Lauten-sack*, 1957, p. 33.

The Hirschvogel attribution dates from a nineteenth-century collector who, on the verso of the page—upon which are drawn several earlier studies of nudes (not illus-trated)—made detailed notes about Hirschvogel. The artistic paternity of this draw-ing is often questioned in the Hirschvogel bibliography. Annegrit Schmitt *(Hanns Lautensack)* nonetheless classifies this drawing as part of the Hirschvogel oeuvre, giving the probable date as 1543, the year when the artist could have passed through Neuburg on a journey from Laibach to Nuremberg. Even before this she was able to identify the site of the drawing as the residence of the Palatine Count Otthein-rich (1502-59). Schmitt considers the view in question to be only partially sketched on the site, since in this landscape, seen from the northern bank of the Danube, the spires of the town churches are too close to one another.

HANS BALDUNG GRIEN

Painter, engraver, and designer of woodcuts and windows. Born 1484-85 in Schwä-bisch Gmünd. Died in Strasburg in 1545.

BIBLIOGRAPHY: G. v. Térey, *Die Handzeichnungen des Hans Baldung, gen. Grien*, 3 vols., 1894-96; O. Fischer, *Hans Baldung Grien*, 2nd ed., 1943; C. Koch, *Die Zeichnungen Hans Baldung Griens*, 1941; *Hans Baldung Grien*, exhibition in the Staatliche Kunsthalle Karlsruhe, 1959 (catalogue).

83. *The Beheading of St. Barbara*

Pen and black ink. Watermark: tall crown (see Briquet 4854 ff.). 294 x 208 mm, $11\frac{1}{2}$ x $8\frac{1}{8}$ in. Dated 1505.

Coll. Liphart and Rodrigues (Lugt 897). Acquired 1921. KdZ 11716.

BIBLIOGRAPHY: *Société de reproductions des dessins de Maîtres*, vol. 4, 1921, pl. 24; K. T. Parker, "Elsässische Handzeichnungen des 15. und 16. Jahrhunderts," *Die Meisterzeichnung* 2, 1928, no. 27; Fischer, p. 16; Koch, no. 6; *Baldung-Aus-stellung*, no. 105; *Meister um Albrecht Dürer*, no. 9; K. Oettinger-K. A. Knappe, *Hans Baldung-Grien und A. Dürer in Nürnberg*, 1963, no. 24.

This drawing was executed during Baldung Grien's sojourn in Dürer's studio. In the figure of the executioner specific borrowings from the executioner in Dürer's wood-cut *Martyrdom of St. Catherine* (B.120) and from the lansquenets in the *Large Passion* are easily discernible. The landscape too, with its vast stretches of water and small round trees, bears witness to a thorough study of Dürer's concept of landscape.

84. *Seated Witch*

Pen and black ink. 183 x 171 mm, 7¼ x 6¾ in. Inscribed with monogram below.

Coll. W. Mitchell (Lugt 2638) and Peart (Lugt 891). In the lower right-hand corner, unknown collector's mark. Acquired 1900. KdZ 4416.

BIBLIOGRAPHY: H. A. Schmid in *RKW* 21, 1898, p. 307; Térey, no. 260; Fried-länder-Bock, p. 9; H. Perseke, *Hans Baldungs Schaffen in Freiburg*, 1941, p. 192; Koch, no. 60; Baldung exhibition, no. 133.

Related to a very similar work in red chalk, also in Berlin, this drawing is generally considered a study for one of Baldung's numerous depictions of witches. The drawing could well date from the beginning of the artist's Freiburg period (around 1513).

85. *Drunken Bacchus*

Pen and brush with black ink, heightened with white on brown tinted paper. 333 x 233 mm, 13⅛ x 9⅛ in. Monogram and the date 1517.

Part of the original collection. KdZ 289.

BIBLIOGRAPHY: O. Eisenmann in *J. Meyers Allgemeines Künstlerlexikon*, vol. 2, 1878, pp. 617 ff.; Lippmann-Grote, 2nd ed., no. 160; Térey, no. 48; Friedländer-Bock, p. 10; K. T. Parker, "Elsässische Handzeichnungen des 15. und 16. Jahr-hunderts," *Die Meisterzeichnung* 2, 1928, no. 34; F. Winkler, *Hans Baldung Grien, Ein unbekannter Meister deutscher Zeichnung*, 1939, p. 20, no. 24; Koch, no. 104; H. Perseke, *Hans Baldungs Schaffen in Freiburg*, 1941, no. 18; Baldung exhibition, no. 154.

The artist probably derived the theme of this drawing from North Italian models, perhaps from engravings of the Mantegna circle. The frame, drawn by the artist, confers a finished quality upon the drawing that corresponds with the detailed execution. The work must have been conceived after the completion of the main altar-piece of the Cathedral of Freiburg, in the beginning of 1517 after the artist's return to Strasburg. This drawing is situated between the pen and ink drawing which the artist made for the prayer book of Maximilian (Koch no. 53, about 1515), and the woodcut of a *Sleeping Bacchus* (B.45), which today is considered to date from the first half of the 1520's.

86. *A Lady at Prayer*

Charcoal and red chalk. 395 x 308 mm, 15½ x 12⅛ in. Monogram added later at the upper left within the date 1519.

Coll. Esdail (Lugt 2617). KdZ 296.

BIBLIOGRAPHY: A. Woltmann in *JKW* 4, 1871, pp. 354 ff.; Térey, no. 42; R. Stiassny in *Kunstchronik*, n.s. 5, 1893-94, pp. 137 ff.; Friedländer-Bock, p. 10; Koch, no. A 1.

The woman portrayed here bears a strong resemblance to the donor depicted in the right wing of the St. John altar in Frankfurt (see cat. 87). Although this drawing has elicited admiration from other writers, Koch does not accept its attribution to Baldung. If it is by him it is his only known drawing executed in red chalk. The signature is also open to question. The truncated headdress leads us to conclude that the drawing was originally larger, and the fold, now in the upper portion of the sheet, is another argument in favor of the hypothesis that the upper margin was cut down. The date could have been transferred there by an unknown hand after the page had been cut, or added later. The technique of the drawing recalls the *Praying Donor* in Berlin (Koch no. 130). The weakness of the line, criticized by Koch, seems to have been caused principally by careless rubbing of the page.

87. *Portrait of a Burgher's Wife Wearing a Coif*

Silverpoint. 141 x 99 mm, 5½ x 3⅞ in. Signed with monogram.

Coll. Hausmann (Lugt 377). Acquired 1875. KdZ 300.

BIBLIOGRAPHY: Térey, no. 141; R. Stiassny, *Wappenzeichnungen Hans Baldung Griens in Coburg*, 1895, p. 64; Térey in *RKW* 18, 1896, p. 475; Friedländer-Bock, p. 9; Koch, no. 160; Baldung exhibition, no. 161.

In 1896 Térey had recognized that this drawing was a life study for the donor portrait of Frau von Gottesheim of Hagenau (Alsace). She appears in the *Baptism of Christ* on the left wing of the St. John altar in Frankfurt (1519-20). On the verso are five caricatures of heads seen in profile.

88. *Young Girl Wearing a Necklace*

Silverpoint. 124 x 86 mm, 4⅞ x 3⅜ in. Signed with monogram.

Coll. Hausmann (Lugt 377). Acquired 1875. KdZ 301.

BIBLIOGRAPHY: Térey, no. 39; Friedländer-Bock, p. 9; Koch, no. 161; *Winkler Altdeutsche Zeichnungen*, p. 50; Baldung exhibition, no. 162.

Koch dates this drawing (also cat. 87) in the vicinity of 1520. The monogram was probably added by the Strasburg chronicler Sebaldus Büheler. The latter had received the contents of Baldung's studio from his sister, widow of the Strasburg painter Nikolaus Kremer.

89. *Venus with an Apple*

Pen and brown ink. Watermark: variant of Briquet 4968. 298 x 166 mm, 11¾ x 6½ in.

Coll. King Friedrich-Wilhelm I (Lugt 1631). KdZ 2171.

BIBLIOGRAPHY: Térey, no. 29; Friedländer-Bock, p. 10; L. Baldass in *MJBK*, n.s. 3, 1926, p. 16; F. Winkler, *H. Baldung Grien, ein unbekannter Meister deutscher Zeichnung*, 1939, pp. 15 ff.; Koch, no. 126; Baldung exhibition, no. 167.

This drawing obviously represents Venus holding the apple, prize of the victory conferred upon her by Paris. Nevertheless, the subject has also been identified as Eve, or simply, as in the Berlin catalogue, a study of a nude. The resemblance to the young sorceress in the Frankfurt painting *Two Weather Witches* of 1523 leads us to suppose this drawing to be of the same period and drawn from the same model. A copy, contours only, is in Coburg.

90. *Masquerade before an Island Castle*

Pen and brown ink, heightened with wash. 378 x 277 mm, 14⅞ x 10⅞ in. Monogram at the lower left added later by an unknown hand.

Coll. Ottley, Esdail (Lugt 2617), and v. Rumohr (Lugt 2160). KdZ 801.

BIBLIOGRAPHY: Térey, no. 13; Friedländer-Bock, p. 10; L. Baldass in *MJBK*, n.s. 3, 1926, p. 42; Koch, no. 132; H. Möhle in *ZKG* 10, 1941-42, pp. 214 ff.; Baldung exhibition, no. 173.

The monogram was added by S. Büheler. Koch thinks that this still unexplained scene may have been inspired by a poem. He places its execution in the vicinity of 1530 (cf. cat. 88).

91. *Sketch for a Window Bearing the Arms of the Strasburg Family of Böcklin von Böcklinsau*

Pen and black ink with gray wash. 357 x 258 mm, 14 x 10⅛ in. Dated in the lower center, 1534.

Coll. Savigny. Acquired 1925. KdZ 12.286.

BIBLIOGRAPHY: K. T. Parker, "Elsässische Handzeichnungen des 15. and 16. Jahrhunderts," *Die Meisterzeichnung* 2, 1928, no. 44; F. Winkler, *Hans Baldung Grien. Ein unbekannter Meister deutscher Zeichnung*, 1939, p. 23, no. 32; Koch, no. 159; Baldung exhibition, no. 245.

Parker was the first to publish this drawing, at which time he favored a definite Baldung attribution, although the latter's authorship was doubted by the Berlin Print Room. The design was probably made for Philipp Böcklin von Böcklinsau.

HANS LEU

Painter and designer of woodcuts. Born in Zurich around 1490. Killed in the Battle on the Gubel, October 24, 1531.

92. *The Rest on the Flight into Egypt*

Pen and black ink with wash, heightened with white on brown tinted paper. 280 x 202 mm, 11 x 8 in. Signed with monogram at the upper right and dated 1521.

Coll. Major. Acquired 1897. KdZ 4066.

BIBLIOGRAPHY: Lippmann-Grote, 2nd ed., no. 194; Ganz, *Handzeichnungen*, III, p. 51; Friedländer-Bock, p. 63; Friedländer-Bock, *Handzeichnungen*, pl. 98; W. Hugelshofer in *ASAK*, n.s., 26, 1924, pp. 122 ff.; Id., *Die Züricher Malerei bis zum Ausgang der Spätgotik*, 1st part (*Mitteilungen d. Antiquarischen Gesellschaft in Zürich*, vol. 30, no. 4), 1928, p. 56; Id., "Schweizer Handzeichnungen des 15. und 16. Jahrhunderts," *Die Meisterzeichnung* 1, 1928, no. 37.

This page, highly reminiscent of Baldung Grien, shows certain weaknesses in the drawing. The expression on the Virgin's face is almost obliterated by the very dark wash. One can see the artist's efforts to create a finished work. The manner of placing the figures in the immediate foreground of the scene is characteristic of Leu's style of composition.

HEINRICH ALDEGREVER

Painter and engraver. Born in 1502 in Paderborn. Active in Soest where he died in 1555.

93. *Half-Length Portrait of a Man*

Black and colored chalk. 272 x 184 mm, 10¾ x 7¼ in. An inscription, almost entirely erased, on the lower edge.

Acquired 1903. KdZ 4242.

BIBLIOGRAPHY: Lippmann-Grote, 2nd ed., no. 204; Thieme-Becker, I, p. 241; Friedländer-Bock, p. 3; Friedländer-Bock, *Handzeichnungen*, pl. 53; F. Winkler, "Mittel-, niederrheinische und westfälische Handzeichnungen des 15. und 16. Jahrhunderts," *Die Meisterzeichnung* 4, 1932, no. 66; R. Fritz in *BM*, n.s. 10, 1961, pp. 15 ff.

R. Fritz has proved conclusively that this drawing is the self-portrait of the Westphalian painter and engraver Heinrich Aldegrever, done when he was about thirty-eight. The dating of the drawing in the vicinity of 1540 is based upon a comparison with the engraved self-portrait of 1537 (B.189), which seems to show the artist several years younger.

BERNHARD STRIGEL

Painter. Born in 1460 or 1461 in Memmingen, where he died on May 4, 1528.

94. *Doubting Thomas*

Pen and brush with black ink, heightened with white on red tinted paper. 379 x 272 mm, 14⅞ x 10⅝ in. Signed below with monogram on a small tablet.

Coll. Mayor (Lugt 2799) and v. Beckerath (Lugt 2504). Acquired 1902. KdZ 5548.

BIBLIOGRAPHY: Lippmann-Grote, 2nd ed., no. 197; Friedländer-Bock, p. 95; K. T. Parker-W. Hugelshofer in *Belvedere* 8, 1925, pp. 29 ff.

There survive little more than a dozen drawings that can be attributed with any degree of certainty to this extraordinarily productive painter. In spite of certain weaknesses in the drawing Hugelshofer considers this the most beautiful of Strigel's work, dating the page in the vicinity of 1510. The monogram on the cartouche has been wrongly interpreted as that of Hans Goldschmid, a pupil of Strigel.

HANS HOLBEIN THE ELDER

Painter and designer of woodcuts and windows. Born in Augsburg around 1465. Active in Augsburg and Basel. Died in 1524 in Isenheim (Alsace).

> BIBLIOGRAPHY: A. Woltmann, *Holbein und seine Zeit*, vol. 2, 2nd ed., 1874-76; Id., *Hans Holbein d.Ä., Silberstift Zeichnungen im K. Museum z. Berlin*, 1876; J. E. Weis-Liebersdorf, "Kirchliche Kunst im alten Augsburg," in *Das Jubeljahr 1500 in der Augsburger Kunst*, 1901; C. Glaser, *H. Holbein d.Ä.*, 1908; N. Lieb-A. Stange, *H. Holbein d.Ä.*, 1960; *Die Malerfamilie Holbein*.

95. *The Martyrdom of St. Paul*

> Pen and brown ink, with India ink. 446 x 260 mm, 17½ x 10¼ in. Completed in the upper portion by restoration.
>
> Coll. King Friedrich-Wilhelm I (Lugt 1631). KdZ 2305.
>
> BIBLIOGRAPHY: H. Janitschek, *Geschichte d. deutschen Malerei;* Glaser, no. 264; Friedländer-Bock, p. 47; Lieb-Stange, pp. 39, 65, 94.

This drawing shows the beheading of the Apostle Paul outside the walls of Rome, where later the Basilica of St. Paul Outside-the-Walls was to stand. Above this scene the artist depicted Christ Crowned with Thorns. The page corresponds in every detail to the central panel of the painting the *Basilica of St. Paul*, now in the museum in Augsburg (Lieb-Stange no. 24a, pl. 88). This panel is one of a series representing the origins of the major Roman basilicas. It decorated one of the bays of the ogival walls of the chapter room of the Dominican Convent of St. Catherine in Augsburg. Glaser describes the Berlin drawing as a "weak imitation," a point of view which is echoed by the equally hesitant attitude of Lieb and Stange. In the text volume of their work (pp. 38-39), the drawing is classified among the works that should serve as a point of departure for establishing a list of authentic drawings, while conversely, in the catalogue volume (p. 83) it is listed as a studio piece. The drawing in question was probably made in the workshop preparatory to the painting, which was executed around 1504 for the series of the *Roman Basilicas*, commissioned by the Abbess Veronika Welser.

96. Recto: *Duke Charles of Burgundy as a Child (Charles V)*

Silverpoint. 151 x 92 mm, 5⅞ x 3⅝ in. Inscribed with red pencil: "hertzog karl vō burgundy."

Coll. v. Nagler (Lugt 2529). KdZ 2510.

Verso: *The Duke's Hand Holding the Falcon (detail)*

Inscribed in red pencil: "kaisers falck."

BIBLIOGRAPHY: Woltmann, no. 110, vol. 1, p. 69; Id., *Berliner Zeichnungen*, pl. 7; Glaser, no. 134; Friedländer-Bock, p. 48; L. Baldass in *Buchner-Feuchtmayr*, vol. 2, p. 179; Lieb-Stange, nos. 119-120.

This work is not a life study but a drawing after a Netherlandish painting, copies of which survive in Trier and Vienna. Since the Vienna painting is dated 1507 we can place the drawing close to this date.

97. *Portrait of Jakob Fugger*

Silverpoint. The face and cap have been reworked with brush and pen and ink. 134 x 93 mm, 5¼ x 3⅝ in. Inscribed in ink by an unknown hand: Jacob Fuckher. On the verso is the probable authentic inscription: Her Jacob Fuger vo Augspurgk.

Coll. v. Nagler (Lugt 2529). Acquired 1835. KdZ 2518.

BIBLIOGRAPHY: Woltmann, no. 118; Id., *Berliner Zeichnungen*, pl. 42; Weis-Liebersdorf, fig. 15; Glaser, 138; Friedländer-Bock, p. 48; N. Lieb, *Die Fugger und die Kunst im Zeitalter der Spätgotik und frühen Renaissance*, 1952, p. 16; Id., *Die Fugger und die Kunst im Zeitalter der hohen Renaissance*, 1958, pp. 478 ff.; Lieb-Stange, no. 263.

Another, more schematic version of this portrait of the renowned Augsburg merchant is in Copenhagen, but it accords from all points of view with the Berlin drawing. The Copenhagen drawing is dated 1509.

Jakob Fugger the Rich (1459-1525) was the most important banker of the sixteenth century. He contributed largely—by a loan of more than 500,000 florins—to the election of Charles V as Emperor of Germany.

98. *The Emperor Maximilian on Horseback*

Silverpoint, heightened with white. 154 x 94 mm, 6 x 3¾ in. Autograph inscription in red pencil: der grosz kaiser maximilian.

Coll. v. Nagler (Lugt 2529). Acquired 1835. KdZ 2509.

BIBLIOGRAPHY: Woltmann, no. 109, vol. 1, pp. 67 ff.; Id., *Berliner Zeichnungen*, pl. 37; Weis-Liebersdorf, fig. 12; Glaser, no. 139; L. Baldass in *JKSAK* 31, 1914, p. 290; Friedländer-Bock, p. 48; H. A. Schmid, *Die Werke H. Holbeins (d.J.) in Basel*, 1930, p. 19; O. Benesch in *ZBK* 64, 1930-31, p. 39; E. Schilling, *Alt-deutsche Meisterzeichnungen*, 1934, p. 13; Id., *Zeichnungen d. Künstlerfamilie Holbein*, 2nd ed., 1954, p. 14; *Kaiser Maximilian I*, cat. of Vienna exhibition, 1959, p. 135; N. Lieb, *Jakob Fugger, Kaiser Maximilian und Augsburg*, 1959, p. 61; Lieb-Stange, no. 158.

The Emperor Maximilian, in general fond of great luxury, nonetheless liked occasionally to ride clad in rather simple attire such as hunting costumes. Götz v. Berlichingen thus relates in his memoirs that having encountered the Emperor in Constance during the Swiss War of 1499, he was only able to recognize him by his large nose, since, unlike those in his retinue, he was clad in an almost shabby hunting costume. Holbein's drawing was probably made during one of the Diets, in 1510 or 1513.

99. *Portrait of Kunz von der Rosen*

Silverpoint. The face and beard have been reworked with a brush. 98 x 89 mm, 3⅞ x 3½ in. Inscription in ink, probably by a later hand: Cuntz v der Rosen.

Coll. v. Nagler (Lugt 2529). Acquired 1835. KdZ 2511.

BIBLIOGRAPHY: Woltmann, no. 111; Id., *Berliner Zeichnungen*, pl. 11; Weis-Liebersdorf, fig. 13; Glaser, no. 135; Friedländer-Bock, p. 48; Lieb-Stange, no. 272.

This drawing is the second stage of a small sketch, also in Berlin (KdZ 2512). Judging from the position of the head the drawing exhibited here may have provided the model for Daniel Hopfer's etching *Portrait of Kunz von der Rosen* (B.87). The identity of the sitter has sometimes been questioned. But as the same person is portrayed under the name of Kunz von der Rosen in a miniature on parchment (destroyed during the war) by the Augsburg artist Narziss Renner, there can be no doubt as to the identity of the subject.

Kunz (Konrad) von der Rosen (ca. 1455-1519), the "joyous councillor" of Emperor Maximilian, was a native of Kaufbeuren and had been in the prince's service since 1478. He was imprisoned with Maximilian in Bruges in 1488.

100. *The Artist's Sons, Ambrosius and Hans*

Silverpoint. 103 x 155 mm, 4 x 6⅛ in. Date and inscription in the artist's hand:

1511   14

prosy   Hanns

Holbain

The indication of age above Ambrosius' head has been destroyed. The face of Hans has been retouched with pen.

Coll. v. Nagler (Lugt 2529). Acquired 1835. KdZ 2507.

BIBLIOGRAPHY: Woltmann, no. 107, vol. 1, pp. 61 ff., vol. 2, pp. 73 ff.; Id., *Berliner Zeichnungen*, no. 39; E. His, *H. Holbein d.Ä. Silberstiftzeichnungen*, 1885, p. 5; H. Knackfuss, *H. Holbein d.J.*, 1896, p. 1; A. Philippi, *Die Kunst d. 15. u. 16. Jahrhunderts in Deutschland und den Niederlanden*, 1898, fig. 86; Weis-Liebersdorf, pp. 41 ff.; Lippmann-Grote, 2nd ed., no. 169; Glaser, no. 153; W. Hes, *Ambrosius Holbein*, 1911, pl. 1; P. Ganz, *H. Holbein d.J.*, 1912, p. 12; Friedländer-Bock, p. 48; Thieme-Becker XVII, pp. 327, 331, 336; E. Schilling in *P* 12, 1933, p. 322; Id., *Altdeutsche Meisterzeichnungen*, 1934, p. 13; Id., *Zeichnungen d. Künstlerfamilie Holbein*, 1st ed. 1937 (2nd ed. 1954), p. 11; W. Pinder, *Die deutsche Kunst der Dürerzeit*, 1940, fig. 92; H. A. Schmid, *H. Holbein d.J.*, 1945-48, p. 13; N. Lieb in *Lebensbilder aus dem Bayerischen Schwaben*, vol. 1, 1952, p. 178; H. W. Grohn, *H. Holbein d.J. als Maler*, 1955, pp. 9 ff.; *Augusta 955-1955*, pl. 81; Lieb-Stange, no. 237.

Holbein has admirably conveyed here the difference in character of his two sons: the elder, Ambrosius (born in 1490), soft-featured and romantic, and the younger, Hans, energetic. According to the ages indicated this drawing can be placed around the years 1511-12. Ambrosius left Augsburg in 1514, Hans in 1515, both subsequently working for a time in Basel.

101. *Portrait of Sigmund Holbein*

Silverpoint, heightened with red and white. 134 x 102 mm, 5¼ x 4 in. Inscribed in ink by an unknown hand: Sigmund Holbain maler. Several lines retraced at a later date. On the verso: notes and a sketch of a coat of arms.

Coll. v. Nagler (Lugt 2529). Acquired 1835. KdZ 2508.

BIBLIOGRAPHY: Woltmann, no. 108, vol. 1, p. 66, vol. 2, pp. 55 ff.; Id., *Berliner Zeichnungen*, pl. 1; Glaser, no. 151; Friedländer-Bock, p. 48; E. Buchner, "*Zum Werk H. Holbein d.Ä.*," in *Buchner-Feuchtmayer*, vol. 2, p. 396; E. Schilling in *P.* 12, 1933, p. 322; Id., *Zeichnungen d. Künstlerfamilie Holbein*, 2nd ed., 1954, p. 10; P. Strieder, *Der ältere Holbein*, 1947, fig. 17; N. Lieb in *Lebensbilder aus dem Bayerischen Schwaben*, vol. 1, 1952, p. 177; E. Buchner in *MJBK* 3.6, 1955, p. 160; Lieb-Stange, no. 227; *Die Malerfamilie Holbein in Basel*, no. 34.

Sigmund, the younger brother of Hans Holbein the Elder, worked in the latter's studio from 1497 until he established himself as master painter in Augsburg in 1503. He left for Switzerland in 1518 and died in Bern in 1540. A second version of this drawing, formerly in the Malcolm collection, is now in the British Museum. There is also a copy in Düsseldorf. The London drawing served as model for the engraved portrait of Sandrart in *Teutsche Academie der Bau- Bild- und Mahlereikünste*, 1675.

102. *Portrait of Leonhard Wagner*

Silverpoint on reddish tinted paper. Heavily reworked with brush and pen in black and opaque white. 136 x 96 mm, 5⅜ x 3¾ in. Inscribed in ink by an unknown hand: Her Leonhard Wagner. Above: an arithmetic calculation by the artist in silverpoint.

Coll. v. Nagler (Lugt 2529). Acquired 1835. KdZ 2524.

BIBLIOGRAPHY: Woltmann, no. 124; Id., *Berliner Zeichnungen*, pl. 20; Glaser, no. 100; A. Schröders, *Archiv für die Geschichte des Hochstifts Augsburg*, vol. 1, 1909-11, p. 372; Friedländer-Bock, p. 49; E. Steingräber, *Die kirchliche Buchmalerei Augsburgs um 1500*, 1956, p. 49; Lieb-Stange, no. 186.

Father Leonhard Wagner was a monk in the Benedictine abbey of Sts. Ulrich and Afra, in Augsburg. A calligrapher of renown, his contribution to the formation of German Gothic script was essential. Holbein used this portrait for the head of St. Ulrich in the painting *St. Ulrich and the Miracle of the Fishes*, painted in 1512 (Lieb-Stange, no. 31 d, pl. 105).

103. *Portrait of Jörg Schenck zum Schenkenstein*

Silverpoint. 134 x 93 mm, 5¼ x 7⅝ in. Facial contours gone over. Inscription in ink by an unknown hand: Jerg Schenck zum Schenkensta[in].

Coll. v. Nagler (Lugt 2529). Acquired 1835. KdZ 2547.

BIBLIOGRAPHY: Woltmann, no. 147, vol. 1, p. 71; Id., *Berliner Zeichnungen*, pl. 18; Glaser, no. 171; Friedländer-Bock, p. 50; *Deutsche Zeichnungen 1400-1900*, no. 74; *Die Malerfamilie Holbein in Basel*, no. 31; Winkler, *Altdeutsche Zeichnungen*, p. 46; Lieb-Stange, no. 276.

It is rare in Holbein's work to find a portrait study executed with so much attention to all details. The sitter was probably the Bishop of Augsburg's steward, Hans Schenck zum Schenkenstein, member of a noble Swabian family, who married a woman of Augsburg in 1507.

104. *Portrait of Jörg Bomheckel*

Silverpoint, repainted in color. Face heightened with red and white. 139 x 101 mm, 5½ x 4 in. Lower left corner restored. Autograph inscription, almost completely destroyed: jörg bomheckel. At the left, in somewhat later hand: ... jorigk.

Coll. v. Nagler (Lugt 2529). Acquired 1835. KdZ 2579.

BIBLIOGRAPHY: Woltmann, no. 179; Id., *Berliner Zeichnungen*, pl. 72; Glaser, no. 181; Friedländer-Bock, p. 53; Lieb-Stange, no. 221.

This drawing is one of the rare examples of portrait drawings in which Holbein completed the silverpoint with color. According to Lieb there were two Augsburg weavers by the name of Bomheckel (or a similar name), but neither of them had the given name of Jörg.

105. *Half-Length Portrait of a Man Wearing a Cap*

Silverpoint on chalk background, tinted with red chalk, with white highlights. 136 x 88 mm, 5⅜ x 3½ in. Inscription at the upper left: Haug.

Coll. Campe (Lugt 1391) and Ehlers. Acquired 1938. KdZ 17 660.

BIBLIOGRAPHY: Glaser, no. 208; E. Schilling in *P.* 1933, p. 318; Winkler in *JPKS* 60, 1939, no. 36; Id., *Coll. Ehlers*, no. 2; *Die Weltkunst* 13, 1939, nos. 3-4, p. 3; Lieb-Stange, no. 260.

Lieb and Stange think that the sitter was a member of the Augsburg patrician family Haug. The original inscription was incorrectly read by Winkler as "——anes," which he then hypothetically completed as "Johannes." On the verso is a braided motif, geometrical studies, and an inscription in capital letters.

According to Dr. Wolfgang Pfeiffer, Regensburg, in a note of December 12, 1964, this drawing is probably a study for the painting in the Chrysler Collection, New York (cf. P. Ganz, *H. Holbein d. J.*, Basel, 1950, no. 28, ill. no. 10). However, the subject of the portrait is shown from the other side. Ganz identifies him as the mayor of Basel, Jacob von Hertenstein, 1517.

106. *Portrait of Martin Höfler*

Silverpoint. Face, hair, and cap gone over with pen and ink. 112 x 96 mm, 4⅜ x 3¾ in. Inscribed in ink by an unknown hand: martin d fuckher diener.

Coll. v. Nagler (Lugt 2529). Acquired 1835. KdZ 2523.

BIBLIOGRAPHY: *Woltmann*, no. 123; Id., *Berliner Zeichnungen*, pl. 41; Glaser, no. 176; Friedländer-Bock, p. 49; N. Lieb, *Die Fugger und die Kunst der Spätgotik und frühen Renaissance*, 1952, pp. 63, 341; Id., *Die Fugger und die Kunst der hohen Renaissance*, 1958, p. 478; Lieb-Stange, no. 277.

Martin Höfler was employed in the Fugger enterprises.

107. *Study of Hands*

Silverpoint. Three of the hands gone over with ink and red crayon. 185 x 139 mm, 7¼ x 5½ in.

Coll. v. Nagler (Lugt 2529). Acquired 1835. KdZ 2580.

BIBLIOGRAPHY: Glaser, no. 219; Friedländer-Bock, p. 53; Lieb-Stange, no. 144.

Hans Holbein the Elder made a prodigious number of life studies using silverpoint. There are studies of hands by Holbein in Basel and Copenhagen as well. No one has been able to establish any correlation between the Berlin study and one of the artist's paintings.

AMBROSIUS HOLBEIN

Painter and designer of woodcuts. Born around 1494 in Augsburg. Son of Hans Holbein the Elder. Known to have been in Basel until 1519.

108. *Portrait of a Young Man*

Silverpoint on white tinted paper. 182 x 132 mm, 7⅛ x 5¼ in. Corners cut, with traces of a signature at the upper left.

Part of the original collection. KdZ 298.

BIBLIOGRAPHY: Lippmann-Grote, 2nd ed., no. 159; G. von Térey, *Die Handzeichnungen des H. Baldung Grien*, vol. 1, 1894, pl. 43, vol. 3, 1896, p. XCVII, no. 11; Friedländer-Bock, p. 11; Friedländer-Bock, *Handzeichnungen*, p. 57; E. Koegler in *Thieme-Becker* XVII, p. 329; *Die Malerfamilie Holbein*, no. 101.

Térey published this drawing in 1894 as a work by Hans Baldung. But in 1896, in the text volume of his book, he proposed Ambrosius as the author of the drawing. The work does seem closest to this artist's style of drawing, although his particular artistic qualities do not yet emerge clearly. Among the portrait drawings and paintings from the second decade of the sixteenth century especially are various works sometimes attributed to Ambrosius or to his younger brother, Hans.

HANS HOLBEIN THE YOUNGER

Painter, designer of woodcuts. Son of Hans Holbein the Elder. Born in Augsburg, probably at the end of 1497. Left for Basel in 1515. Travels in Northern Italy in 1516-17 and in France in 1524. First sojourn in England in 1526-28, after which he returned to Basel. Settled finally in England in 1532 where he became, in 1536, court painter to Henry VIII. Died in London in 1543.

BIBLIOGRAPHY: A. Woltmann, *Hans Holbein und seine Zeit*, 2 vols., 2nd ed., 1873-76; E. His, *Dessins d'ornaments de H. Holbein le Jeune*, 1886; P. Ganz, *Handzeichnungen Hans Holbeins in Auswahl*, 1908; P. Ganz, *Die Handzeichnungen H. Holbeins d.J., Kritischer Katalog*, 1911-1937; P. Ganz, "Hans Holbein d.J. Des Meisters Gemälde," *Klassiker der Kunst*; H. A. Schmid in Thieme-Becker XVII; W. Waetzoldt, *H. Holbein d.J., Werk und Welt*, 1938; H. A. Schmid, *Hans Holbein d.J. Sein Aufstieg zur Meisterschaft und sein englischer Stil*, 3 vols., 1945-48; *Die Malerfamilie Holbein in Basel*, exhibition at the Kunstmuseum of Basel for 500th anniversary celebrations of the University of Basel, 1960.

109. *Project for the Fresco Decoration on the Facade of the "Haus zum Tanz," Basel*

Pen and ink, heightened with watercolor. 571 x 339 mm, 22½ x 13⅜ in.

Acquired from Karlsruhe. KdZ 3104.

BIBLIOGRAPHY: Woltmann, p. 119, no. 118; His, no. 24; Ganz, 1911-1937, no. 113; Id., *Klassiker der Kunst*, p. 160; Friedländer-Bock, p. 54; Ganz, *Die Malerfamilie Holbein in Basel*, no. 266.

Holbein was probably commissioned about 1520 by the goldsmith Balthasar Angelrot to execute frescoes on the facade of his house in Basel. The "Haus zum Tanz" was located on the corner of the Tanzgasse in the little Eisengasse, which led to the Rhine bridge. Thanks to the number of studies which survive, mostly in copies, it is possible to formulate a composite picture of these frescoes. The Berlin drawing is a study for the decoration of the narrow central facade on the Eisengasse. Until now no research has been able to establish firmly whether this drawing and the copy in Basel—which is somewhat weaker, signed "H.L." and dated "1520"—both derive from a lost original, or whether the Berlin drawing should be considered the original work. Paul Ganz has shown convincingly that the Berlin study was a working drawing. This would explain, even in the case of a sketch by Holbein's own hand, the hesitations and general lifelessness of the line. We agree with the catalogue of the Holbein Exhibition in Basel (p. 29) that this fresco study should be viewed as an early work which preceded the official commission for the decoration of the council chamber in Basel. This hypothesis seems confirmed by Holbein's apparent statement, during his final sojourn in Basel in 1538, that of all his mural paintings only those for the "Haus zum Tanz" were of fairly high quality. A more schematic sketch (*Die Malerfamilie Holbein in Basel*, no. 269), formerly considered a preliminary drawing, is today correctly seen as a more rigorous, later version. Of the actual frescoes for the "Haus zum Tanz" nothing survives. A reconstruction may be found in P. Ganz, *Hans Holbein der Jüngere*, 1950, no. 162, ill. 41.

110. *Two Lansquenets Bearing an Escutcheon*

Pen and black ink with watercolor. 457 x 365 mm, 18 x 14⅜ in.

Coll. v. Nagler (Lugt 2529). Acquired 1835. KdZ 3103.

BIBLIOGRAPHY: Woltmann, vol. 1, p. 119; His, no. 15; P. Ganz, *Auswahl*, p. 32; Id., *Kritischer Katalog*, no. 121; Th. von Liebenau, *H. Holbein d.J. Fresken am Hertensteinhause in Luzern*, 1888, p. 129, note 1; Ganz, *Handzeichnungen*, III, 36; Friedländer-Bock, p. 54; Schmid in Thieme-Becker XVII, p. 338; Id., *H. Holbein d.J.*, vol. 1, pp. 15 and 81; W. Cohn, *Der Wandel der Architekturgestaltung in den Werken H. Holbeins d.J.*, 1930, pp. 18 ff.; *Die Malerfamilie Holbein*, no. 163.

By its style this drawing for an armorial window, commissioned by an unknown patron, must be dated 1523-24. Windows of this type were in general use from the mid-fifteenth century and were particularly common in the Swiss cantons, where from about 1500 on their ever-increasing production may be traced. Holbein's numerous studies unquestionably constitute the culminating point of the infatuation for painted windows.

111. *Parnassus*

Brush with black ink, lightly gone over with watercolor on brown tinted paper. 421 x 384 mm, 16½ x 15⅛ in. All four corners cut.

Coll. Crozat and Weigel (Lugt 2554). Acquired 1885. KdZ 3105.

BIBLIOGRAPHY: Weigel, *Handzeichnungen berühmter Meister*, pl. 34; Id., *Ähren-lese*, no. 2131; Woltmann, no. 175; Ganz, *Auswahl*, p. 48, no. 30; Id. *Kritischer Katalog*, no. 121; Id., *Klassiker der Kunst*, p. 178; Friedländer-Bock, p. 54; Waetzoldt, pp. 112, 189; Schmid, *H. Holbein d.J.*, vol. 1, p. 393; E. Schilling, *Zeichnungen der Künstlerfamilie Holbein*, 2nd ed., 1954, pp. 18 ff.; *Deutsche Zeichnungen 1400-1900*, no. 83.

Apollo and the Muses are shown here on Parnassus. Apollo is sheltered by a balda-quin ornamented with an imperial eagle. The composition was commissioned by the German merchants of London to decorate the "Stahlhof" on the occasion of Queen Anne Boleyn's triumphal entry following her coronation in 1553. From the accounts of Charles V's ambassadors and other eyewitnesses, we may conclude that this decoration was actually constructed in a similar manner. The composition sketched by Holbein may have been presented as a *tableau vivant*, as was often done on the continent. It is said that all day during the procession Rhine wine flowed from the spring of Castalia at the feet of Apollo.

HANS BURGKMAIR THE ELDER

Painter, designer of woodcuts. Born in Augsburg in 1473, died there in 1531.

BIBLIOGRAPHY: H. A. Schmid in Thieme-Becker V, 1911; H. Rupé, *Beiträge zum Werke H.B.d.Ä.* (Diss. Freiburg), 1912; *Burgkmair-Ausstellung in der Staat-lichen Gemäldegalerie zu Augsburg*, 1931; A. Burkhard, *Hans Burgkmair*, 1934; P. Halm in *MJBK* 3 F., 13, 1962, pp. 75 ff.

112. *Christ on the Mount of Olives*

Pen and brown ink. 233 x 199 mm, 9⅛ x 7⅞ in. Rounded above. Signed with monogram on the pedestal.

Coll. Weber (Lugt 1383). Acquired 1897. KdZ 4068.

BIBLIOGRAPHY: Springer, *Federzeichnung*, pl. 11; Lippmann-Grote, 2nd ed., no. 193; Schmid, p. 253; Rupé, p. 67, note 1; Friedländer-Bock, p. 18; *Burgkmair-Ausstellung*, no. 34; Burkhard, pp. 44 ff.

This drawing is the preliminary study for an altarpiece, fragments of which are in the Kunsthalle, Hamburg, and in an Italian private collection. The Hamburg frag-ment, which represents Christ praying, is completely signed and dated 1505. Burgkmair had already painted this same subject in 1501. In comparison with that first version the Berlin study shows a more rigorous composition and a greater depth of expression. The structure of the altarpiece is closely related to Italian prototypes. Unfortunately, nothing survives of the predella. The coats of arms indicated at the lower left and right are those of the Augsburg family Rehlinger.

113. *Study Sheet of Horses' Heads and Harnesses*

Charcoal, pen and brown ink, with India ink wash. 318 x 218 mm, 12½ x 8½ in. Toward the bottom center is the inscription: Hanns burgkmair/alles konterfet/. 1516.

Acquired 1878. KdZ 694.

BIBLIOGRAPHY: Rupé, pp. 64 ff.; Schmid, p. 255; Friedländer-Bock, p. 18; *Burgkmair-Ausstellung*, no. 40; Burkhard, p. 116; *Deutsche Zeichnungen 1400-1900*, no. 43.

These studies from nature, freely disposed over the page, were probably executed by Burgkmair as preparatory work for the woodcuts of the *Triumph of the Emperor Maximilian*. Consequently the page may be dated 1515-16. (These woodcuts depict a procession of foot soldiers and cavalry, as was the custom in triumphal entries of the era throughout Europe.) From the explanatory notes we learn that the artist's technical interest in different harnesses accounts for the sample-sheet character of this page. The drawings were first broadly outlined in charcoal, the main details were then elaborated by precisely placed lines in pen and ink, and the drawings finally washed in places with a brush. Burgkmair repeatedly used this fusion of different techniques.

114. *Bust of a Man with a Beard*

Charcoal. 257 x 186 mm, 10⅛ x 7⅜ in. Upper corners cut, lower left corner torn. Dated at the right: 151[9].

Coll. v. Nagler (Lugt 2529). Acquired 1835. KdZ 1260.

BIBLIOGRAPHY: Lippmann-Grote, 2nd ed., no. 175; B. Haendcke, *Schweizerische Malerei des 16. Jahrhunderts*, 1893, pp. 13 and 374; M. J. Friedländer in *RKW* 20, 1897, p. 74; H. A. Schmidt in *JPKS* 19, 1898, p. 74; Friedländer-Bock, p. 18; Winkler, *Altdeutsche Zeichnungen*, p. 48; Burkhard, p. 140.

Between 1517 (*Self-Portrait*, Hamburg) and 1520 (*Portrait of the Artist's Father*, Dresden) Burgkmair worked on a series of large charcoal portraits. It seems likely that it was Dürer's example that led Burgkmair to the use of charcoal for these portraits, as well as influencing him to interpret freely within a large format. By 1503

Dürer had already begun to use charcoal for his portraits and by 1514 had executed several of his most beautiful works in that medium. It is not certain whether the Berlin drawing is actually a portrait, in the strict sense of the word, since a very similar head by the same artist was formerly in the Oppenheimer collection (Lugt 1351; see K. T. Parker, *Drawings of the Early German Schools*, 1926, no. 37). The drawing is probably a portrait study for a more important composition, as the subject's gaze, in particular, seems to suggest.

MATTHÄUS ZASINGER

Goldsmith and engraver. Mentioned in Munich from 1505 to 1514. Councillor in 1512-13. Mentioned in 1507-09 together with Hans Ostendorfer.

115. *Two Knights on Horseback*

> Black chalk. 265 x 372 mm, 10½ x 14⅝ in. Signed MZ. Inscription added later in ink: Matheus Zinck fecit.

> Coll. E. Habich (Lugt 862) and Ehlers. Acquired 1936. KdZ 17 664.

> Bibliography: K. T. Parker in *OMD* 2, 1927-28, pl. 48; Winkler, *Sammlung Ehlers* (cat. of the coll.), p. 17, no. 8; Id. in *JPKS* 60, 1939, no. 24; G. Arnolds in *P.* 23, 1939, pp. 57 ff.

This page is probably a study for a tournament scene. The knight at the left is astride a horse, harnessed for what was called a "German tournament." A figure very similar to the one in the foreground is seen in an engraving by Zasinger, also showing a tournament, and dated 1500. Winkler concludes from this that the drawing could have been conceived shortly thereafter, around 1501-02. The costumes of the two knights suggest, however, a date closer to the second decade of the sixteenth century. The tablet bearing the monogram is borrowed from Dürer woodcuts. Apart from this page, and one in the museum in Nuremberg, no other drawings by Zasinger survive.

SOUTH GERMAN MASTER, ca. 1520

116. *The Virgin on a Crescent Moon, Being Crowned by Angels*

> Pen and black ink. 278 x 178 mm, 11 x 7 in.

Coll. Oppenheimer (Lugt 1351). Acquired 1936. KdZ 16 529.

BIBLIOGRAPHY: K. T. Parker, *Drawings of the Early German Schools*, 1926, no. 48; sale catalogue of the Oppenheimer Collection, London, Christie's, 10-14 July 1936, no. 344; G. Arnolds in *P. 23*, 1939, pp. 57 ff.; Winkler, *Altdeutsche Zeichnungen*, p. 73.

This interesting page is probably a sketch for a window rather than for a woodcut as Parker has suggested. It is difficult to localize. Stylistic similarities to the work of the Upper Rhenish wood sculptor H.L., and to works by Altdorfer and Cranach, indicate a relationship to the Danube School. But a Bavarian or Tyrolean origin is not to be excluded. According to Winkler, Matthäus Zasinger may well have been the author of this drawing (see cat. 115).

JÖRG BREU THE ELDER

Painter and designer of woodcuts and windows, born around 1475-80. Worked initially in Austria. Master Artist in Augsburg from 1502. Influenced by Hans Burgkmair. Died in Augsburg in 1537.

117. *Head of a Young Girl*

Charcoal and red chalk on partially darkened paper. 307 x 221 mm, 12⅛ x 8¾ in. Inscribed with monogram "b" above and dated 1519.

Coll. v. Nagler (Lugt 2529). Acquired 1835. KdZ 803.

BIBLIOGRAPHY: R. Stiassny in *ZCHK* 7, 1894, pp. 101 ff.; Lippmann-Grote, 2nd ed., no. 176; H. Röttinger in Thieme-Becker IV, p. 595; Friedländer-Bock, p. 15; Friedländer-Bock, *Handzeichnungen*, pl. 89; E. Buchner, "Jörg Breu als Maler und Zeichner," in Buchner-Feuchtmayr, vol. 2, p. 339; *Deutsche Zeichnungen 1400-1900*, no. 40.

The treatment of this particularly beautiful page by Breu, generally considered a life study, clearly reveals the influence of Burgkmair's style. The artist utilized this drawing for several paintings; notably, a *Madonna* of 1521 (formerly in the R. v. Kaufmann collection, sale cat., Berlin, P. Cassirer, 1917, vol. 2, fig. 147), and a depiction of *Hell*, in the Museum in Augsburg (Buchner-Feuchtmayr, vol. 2, fig. 245). One may question whether this drawing is really a study after nature. The St. Mary, portrayed in the *Virgin with the Infant Christ, St. Catherine, St. Barbara, and Angels in a Landscape*, a work dated 1512 (formerly in the Gemäldegalerie of Berlin, no. 597 A), is essentially the same facial type.

118. *Roundel Sketch for a Window; Series of the Months: July*

Pen and black ink, with gray wash. Diameter 235 mm, 9¼ in.

Acquired 1928. KdZ 12 839.

119. *Series of the Months: October*

Pen and black ink, with gray wash. Diameter 235 mm, 9¼ in.

Coll. Rodrigues (Lugt 897). Acquired 1897. KdZ 4063.

BIBLIOGRAPHY: Röttinger in Thieme-Becker IV, p. 595; Friedländer-Bock, p. 15; *Ausstellung Augsburger Renaissance*, Augsburg 1955, no. 76.

The Berlin Print Room owns seven pages of this series; there are copies and replicas in different European collections (see J. Baum, *Altschwäbische Kunst*, 1923, fig. 77 ff.). These sketches were later used as models for a series of paintings, also representing the months (see Baum, same references). Thanks to the copy in Bern (Baum, fig. 85) and to a window in Kaiserslautern, scenes of harvest, falconry, and bird catching may be identified as depicting the month of July. In addition, an indication of the month and its zodiac sign appears on the Bern copy. Baum wrongly considers the drawing of coopers (cat. 119) to represent the month of August, but the window in the Augsburg Museum confirms its subject to be October.

MONOGRAMMIST B B

Anonymous Augsburg draftsman of the beginning of the sixteenth century.

BIBLIOGRAPHY: H. Feurstein in *B M* 43, 1922, p. 69; K. Feuchtmayr in *Buchner-Feuchtmayr*, vol. 2, pp. 97 ff.; L. Baldass in *P 4*, 1928, pp. 393 ff.; H. Rott, *Quellen und Forschungen zur Kunstgeschichte im 15. und 16. Jahrhundert*, 3rd part, in 6 vols., 1933-38; F. Winkler, *Augsburger Malerbildnisse der Dürerzeit*, 1948.

120. *Portrait of Jörg Lutz*

Charcoal and pen and ink. 295 x 195 mm, 11⅝ x 7⅝ in. Dated at the upper left in ink: 1513. Signed BB at the lower right. Inscription below in ink: Jörig lutz von . . . ; and to the right the number 19, both on a strip that was formerly pasted to the lower edge of the sheet. On the verso, written in charcoal: Michel Strelin vō nössel.

Coll. Hausmann (Lugt 377). Acquired 1875. KdZ 2020.

BIBLIOGRAPHY: Friedländer-Bock, pp. 67 ff.; Feurstein, p. 71; Feuchtmayr, p. 132, note 1; Baldass, p. 401; Winkler, no. 18; F. Baum, *Meister und Werke spätmittel-alterlicher Kunst in Oberdeutschland und der Schweiz*, 1957, p. 102.

This page is one of a series of twenty charcoal portraits. It has been possible to group them together thanks to the inscription BB in the lower corners, the style of the dates, and in most cases the presence of the sitter's name on a band at the lower edge of the drawing. The monograms, however, were added at a later date, as the portrait of Lutz clearly shows. The letters "BB" were probably meant to indicate Barthel Beham. According to a note by B. Hausmann (Hanover) the twenty sheets were still together in 1812. Today twelve are in Berlin, four in Danzig, two in Hamburg, and one each in Copenhagen and Weimar.

The persons portrayed are most often painters who were working in Augsburg. The presence of Jörg Lutz in that city was documented in 1510. In 1514 he spent time in Bern and Fribourg (Switzerland). In 1546 his death was recorded in Augsburg. Jörg Lutz was the father-in-law of Wilhalm Ziegler (see cat. 122).

121. *Portrait of an Unknown Man*

Charcoal. 265 x 184 mm, 10½ x 7¼ in. Dated 1512. Signed BB at the lower right.

Coll. Hausmann (Lugt 377). Acquired 1875. KdZ 2018.

BIBLIOGRAPHY: Friedländer-Bock, p. 67; Feurstein, p. 71; Feuchtmayr, p. 131, note 1; Baldass, p. 401; Winkler, no. 17.

This charcoal drawing is one of the eight of the series without an inscription bearing the sitter's name. The 3 centimeters (1⅛ in.) missing in the upper portion of the sheet (see cat. 120) indicate that the strip bearing the name has been cut off. This face of a young man with strangely shaped eyes is one of the most appealing portraits in the series.

MONOGRAMMIST IZ OF 1520 (WILHALM ZIEGLER)

The monogrammist IZ is generally identified with the painter Wilhalm Ziegler, who was born around 1480 in Creglingen. He was apprenticed to Hans Burgkmair in 1502 and from 1507 was a burgher of Rotenburg on the Tauber. From 1522 to 1531 he lived in Freiburg in Üchtland and then once again in Rotenburg until 1535.

122. *Portrait of a Young Boy*

Chalk or charcoal. 282 x 180 mm, 11⅛ x 7⅛ in. Signed with a monogram at the right of the head and dated above 1520.

Coll. Campe (Lugt 1391) and Ehlers. Acquired 1938. KdZ 17 689.

BIBLIOGRAPHY: J. Meder in *GK* 31, 1908, p. 38; O. Benesch, *Österr. Handzeich-nungen des 15. und 16. Jahrhunderts* (*Die Meisterzeichnung 5*), 1936, no. 66; F. Winkler, in *JPKS* 60, 1939, no. 42; Id., *Coll. Ehlers*, no. 10; G. Arnolds in *P 23*, 1939, pp. 57 ff.; Winkler, *Altdeutsche Zeichnungen*, p. 56; J. Baum, *Meister und Werke spätmittelalterlicher Kunst in Oberdeutschland und der Schweiz*, 1957, p. 104.

This beautiful drawing has been attributed to both the Salzburg School (Master of the Thenn Portraits) and the Augsburg School. There is a similar drawing in a Swiss private collection (illustrated in G. Swarzenski-E. Schilling, *Handzeichnungen alter Meister in deutschem Privatbesitz*, 1924, pl. 13). Today the tendency is to attribute this work to Wilhalm Ziegler, a pupil of Burgkmair (H. Rott, *Quellen und For-schungen*, vol. 1, p. 54 and vol. 3, pp. 256 ff.). The monogram that appears on the drawings in Berlin and Switzerland is also found on paintings by this itinerant artist.

SOUTH GERMAN MASTER, ca. 1530

123. *Study for a Fountain*

Pen and gray ink, with gray wash. 343 x 202 mm, 13½ x 8 in.

Coll. v. Beckerath (Lugt 2504). Acquired 1902. KdZ 5515.

BIBLIOGRAPHY: Friedländer-Bock, p. 96; Winkler, *Altdeutsche Zeichnungen*, p. 82.

The careful execution of this drawing leads us to consider it a study for an actual fountain. From the fifteenth century on, one finds isolated fountains of this type in Germany. In the sixteenth century this style became very popular: a large basin, with several smaller ones, and numerous orifices for jets of water. A large number of fountains with decorations in the classical style are still seen today in South German cities.

THE MASTER OF MESSKIRCH

Painter active between 1525 and 1550. Takes his name from an altarpiece painted in 1538 in Messkirch for Count Gottfried Werner von Zimmern.

124. *St. Margaret Exorcizing the Dragon*

Pen and black ink, lightly gone over with watercolor. Holes pricked for transfer. 136 x 161 mm, 5⅜ x 6⅜ in.

Coll. Robinson (Lugt 1433). Acquired 1882. KdZ 4266.

BIBLIOGRAPHY: Friedländer-Bock, p. 71; Thieme-Becker, XXXVII, p. 230.

Few drawings survive of this Master, active in the region of Lake Constance. He is still little known as a draftsman, in spite of his great productivity as a painter. The highly delicate tones of watercolor in this work give us a good idea of his painterly style.

DANIEL HOPFER

Painter and etcher. Born in Kaufbeuren. Master Artist in Augsburg from 1493 until his death in 1536.

125. *Tabernacle for the Holy Sacrament*

Pen and brown ink, with wash. Enclosed by charcoal outline. 334 x 157 mm, 13⅛ x 6⅛ in.

Coll. Hausmann (Lugt 378). Acquired 1875. KdZ 2052.

BIBLIOGRAPHY: E. Eyssen, *Daniel Hopfer* (Diss. Heidelberg), 1904, p. 43, no. 7; Friedländer-Bock, p. 56.

This page is a study for the engraving B.127 of Hopfer. He nonetheless made several changes before executing the print. The preparatory drawing, curiously enough, is only partially reversed.

ALBRECHT ALTDORFER

Painter, engraver, etcher, designer of woodcuts, and architect. Born around 1480. Died in Regensburg on February 12, 1538.

BIBLIOGRAPHY: M. J. Friedländer, *Albrecht Altdorfer, der Maler von Regensburg*, 1891; Id., *Albrecht Altdorfer*, 1923; L. Baldass, *Albrecht Altdorfer*, 1923; H. Tietze, *Albrecht Altdorfer*, 1923; M. J. Friedländer, "Die Skizzenbücher," *Albrecht Altdorfer, Ausgewählte Handzeichnungen*, 1923; H. L. Becker, *Die Handzeichnungen Altdorfers*, 1938; L. Baldass, *Albrecht Altdorfer*, 1941; F. Winzinger, *Altdorferzeichnungen*, 1952; K. Oettinger, *Datum und Signatur bei Wolf Huber und Albrecht Altdorfer*, 1957; Id., *Altdorfer-Studien*, 1959.

126. *Landscape with a Pair of Lovers*

Pen and black ink. 282 x 206 mm, 11⅛ x 8⅛ in. Upper left corner and edge cut off. Dated on the left margin [1]504. Signed later at the lower left: Lucas Cran . . . ."

Coll. Suermondt (Lugt 415). Acquired 1874. KdZ 2671.

BIBLIOGRAPHY: M. J. Friedländer in *JPKS* 23, 1902, p. 233 (Cranach); Dornhöffer in *Jb.d.k.k. Zentralkommission Wien*, 2, 1904, p. 186 (Cranach); Voss, *Donaustil*, p. 168 (Cranach); Lippmann-Grote, 2nd ed., no. 193 (Cranach); Friedländer-Bock, p. 19 (Cranach); C. Glaser, *Lucas Cranach*, 1921, pp. 34, 37, 221; Id., *Lucas Cranach d.Ä. Handzeichnungen*, 1922, pp. 10-11, pl. IV; C. Koch, *Zeichnungen altdeutscher Meister zur Zeit Dürers*, 2nd ed., 1923, p. 12 (Cranach); E. Bock in *OMD* 4, 1929-1930, p. 71; M. J. Friedländer-J. Rosenberg, *Die Gemälde von Lucas Cranach*, 1932, p. 4, no. 21 (Cranach); E. Schilling, *Altdeutsche Meisterzeichnungen*, 1934, p. 15 (Cranach); F. Winkler in *B M* 55, 1934, p. 2 (Altdorfer); Th.L. Girshausen, *Die Handzeichnungen Lucas Cranach d.Ä.* (Diss. Frankfurt), 1936, no. 4 (copy by Altdorfer after Cranach); *Altdorfer-Ausstellung*, no. 393 (Cranach); Becker, pp. 74-79 and 125-126; C. Koch in *ZKG* 7, 1938, p. 225 (Cranach); L. Baldass in *JKSW*, n.s. 12, 1938, p. 139; Winzinger, pp. 22-23, notes 16 and 17; Oettinger, *Datum und Signatur*, p. 56 (Altdorfer); Id. in *FKSW* 53 (n.s. 17), 1957, p. 97; Id., *Altdorfer-Studien*, pp. 24, 27 (Altdorfer); J. Rosenberg, *Die Zeichnungen Lucas Cranachs der Ä.*, 1960, no. 7; F. Winzinger in *WJKG* 18 (22), 1960, pp. 7 ff. (Altdorfer).

The authenticity of this drawing is much debated in works concerned with Cranach. Basing his opinion upon the form of the numbers, Winkler convincingly attributes it to Altdorfer. Among the specialists who subsequently studied the drawing, Oettinger and Winzinger share Winkler's opinion. The landscape presents a

number of elements characteristic of Cranach's art, but the draftsmanship is not suf-
ficiently vigorous for that artist's hand. For this reason Hanna Becker thinks the
drawing is a work of Altdorfer after Cranach. Winzinger believes it to be a drawing
by Altdorfer after a Cranach work predating 1500. This opinion, however, is debatable, since, as Oettinger has shown, the motif of the seated couple had its origins
in the Dürer circle.

The drawing reveals in striking fashion the strong influence of Cranach upon the
younger artist, and yet the drawing cannot be considered to be a copy. It also proves
that Altdorfer was familiar with Danube art before settling in Regensburg in 1505.
Benesch was the first to provide documentation in support of this thesis.

127. *Two Women with a Basket of Fruit*

Pen and black ink, heightened with white on tinted red-brown paper. 172 x 123
mm, 6¾ x 4⅞ in. Signed and dated 1506 on the small tablet between the two
figures.

Coll. Hausmann (Lugt 378). Acquired 1875. KdZ 1691.

BIBLIOGRAPHY: Friedländer, 1891, p. 15, no. 1; Voss, *Donaustil*, pp. 117, 171;
Friedländer-Bock, p. 4; L. Baldass, 1923, p. 50; Friedländer, 1923, p. 12; Tietze,
p. 80; Friedländer, *Skizzenbücher*; Becker, no. 3; *Altdorfer-Ausstellung*, no. 66;
Baldass, 1941, p. 37; Winzinger, no. 1; Oettinger, *Datum und Signatur*, p. 15, no.
52; Id., *Altdorfer-Studien*, pp. 23.

Many scholars view this as the earliest surviving drawing by Altdorfer. (Indeed,
only one other drawing, now in the Louvre, is also dated 1506.) The subject has not
yet been thoroughly established. Winzinger's interpretation—"*War Seizing the
Wealth of Peace*"—is, for the moment, the most convincing. According to Winzinger the two figures are probably derived from the engraving of dancing muses
which Zoan Andrea made after Mantegna's painting, *Parnassus*. Early in their ca-
reers Albrecht and Erhard Altdorfer, largely through engravings, came into close
contact with Italian art. The fountain depicted in Erhard's drawing *Banqueters at
a Fountain* (cat. 133), for which Winzinger has recently been able to discover the
Italian sources, constitutes another example of this influence.

128. *St. Margaret Standing upon the Devil*

Pen and black ink, heightened with white on brown toned paper. 159 x 104 mm,
6¼ x 4⅛ in. Signed at the lower right and dated 1509.

Coll. v. Klinkosch (Lugt 577) and v. Lanna. Acquired 1910. KdZ 4466.

BIBLIOGRAPHY: Baldass, 1923, p. 24; Friedländer, 1923, p. 20; Tietze, p. 50; Friedländer-Bock, p. 4; Becker, no. 8; *Altdorfer-Ausstellung*, no. 76; Baldass, 1941, p. 59; Winzinger, no. 18; K. Oettinger, *Datum und Signatur*, p. 16, no. 64; Id., *Altdorfer-Studien*, p. 16.

Around 1509 Altdorfer's style became firmer and more adapted to plastic expression, revealing greater certainty and formal stability in the draftsmanship. The style of the Master of the *Historia Friderici et Maximiliani* (see cat. 134) relates to drawings like this one of St. Margaret.

129. *Samson Vanquishing the Lion*

Pen and black ink, heightened with white on tinted yellow-gray paper. 216 x 155 mm, 8½ x 6⅛ in.

Coll. v. Nagler (Lugt 2529). Acquired 1835. KdZ 86.

BIBLIOGRAPHY: Friedländer, 1891, no. 14; Friedländer-Bock, pp. 4 and 374; Baldass, 1923, p. 69; O. Hagen, *Deutsche Zeichner*, 1921, n. 36; Becker, no. 11; *Altdorfer-Ausstellung*, no. 85; Winzinger, no. 34; K. Oettinger, *Altdorfer-Studien*, p. 48.

The Berlin Print Room owns a copy of this drawing (KdZ 87) as well. An error in interpretation that transformed the jawbone of an ass, hanging from Samson's belt, into a lion's claw, proves that this other drawing, long considered the original, is only a copy. Although the drawing here is unsigned it is generally considered to be by the artist's hand, executed around 1510-12.

130. *The Virgin on a Crescent Moon*

Pen and black ink, heightened with white on tinted gray-green paper. 171 x 118 mm, 6¾ x 4⅝ in. Trimmed all around. At the upper right the date 1518.

Coll. Beurdeley (Lugt 421). Acquired 1920. KdZ 11 601.

BIBLIOGRAPHY: Friedländer-Bock, p. 374; Tietze, p. 138; Friedländer, *Skizzenbücher*, ill. in color; *Altdorfer-Ausstellung*, no. 118; Winzinger, *Studien über die Kunst Altdorfers* (Diss., Munich), 1940, p. 96; C. Koch, *Zeichnungen altdeutscher Meister zur Zeit Dürers*, 2nd ed., 1923, p. 39; G. Lill, H. Leinberger, 1942, pp. 13 ff.; O. Benesch, *Der Maler Albrecht Altdorfer,* 1939, p. 21; Baldass, 1941, p. 14; F. Winzinger in *MJBK* 3 s. 1, 1950, pp. 191 ff.; Winzinger, no. 65; Oettinger, *Datum und Signatur*, p. 18, no. 95; Id., *Altdorfer-Studien*, p. 71.

This drawing represents the *Schöne Maria von Regensburg*, a miraculous Italo-Byzantine statue of the thirteenth century now in the old chapel of Regensburg. This statue was originally in a small chapel. After its transfer in 1519 to a temporary wooden church, built upon the ruins of a demolished synagogue, the statue attracted a vast influx of pilgrims.

Altdorfer executed other woodcuts and engravings of the *Schöne Maria*, among these, a large colored woodcut, of which only a few rare prints survive (B.51). The concept of the drawing is closest to that of the woodcut representing the *Schöne Maria* in a church. This relatively late drawing correctly reproduces the strange character of the Virgin's garment: the *palla* with its hood, fringes and star on the shoulder. A close relationship between this work and a bronze statuette of the *Schöne Maria* by H. Leinberger (Berlin Museum) is easily noticed, as well as a drawing style characteristic of Jörg Kölderer's workshop in Innsbruck.

131. *Landscape with a Large Pine*

Pen and black ink, heightened with gouache and watercolor. 201 x 136 mm, 7⅞ x 5⅜ in. Signed with monogram on the tree trunk.

Part of the original collection. KdZ 11 651.

BIBLIOGRAPHY: Friedländer, 1891, p. 108; L. Baldass, 1923, p. 65; *Die Zeichnungen in der Universitätsbibliothek in Erlangen*, ed. E. Bock, 1929, p. 198; P. Halm in *MJBK*, n.s. 7, 1930, p. 51; Becker, no. 18; *Altdorfer-Ausstellung*, no. 125; O. Benesch, *Der Maler Albrecht Altdorfer*, 1939, p. 26; L. Baldass in *JKSW*, n.s. 12, 1938, pp. 117 ff.; Id., *A. Altdorfer*, 1941, p. 163; Winzinger, no. 67; P. Halm in *ZKW* 8, 1954, p. 82.

The *Landscape with a Pine* is one of Altdorfer's best known drawings, perhaps one of the best known of the whole Dürer period. It is in the same vein as two other Altdorfer landscapes in color (now in Rotterdam and Erlangen). These gouache landscapes are among the latest surviving drawings by this artist and are generally dated 1522. Only one landscape drawing, in pen and ink with watercolor, now in Dresden, bears the date 1524. In theme these drawings are unquestionably related to the large landscape etchings that, as P. Halm has proved (in *ZKW* 8, 1954), were executed between 1520 and 1523. Winzinger (p. 53) quite rightly speaks of miniature landscape, for the technique—watercolor and gouache over a preparatory drawing in pen and ink—relates to German manuscripts of the fifteenth and sixteenth centuries.

132. *Interior of a Church*

Pen and brown ink, with gray wash. 183 x 200 mm, 7¼ x 7⅞ in. Inscription by an unknown hand at the upper left: Albrecht Altdorfer von Regenspurg.

Gift of the van Diemen Art Gallery, 1924. KdZ 11 920.

BIBLIOGRAPHY: E. Bock in *BM* 45, 1924, pp. 12 ff.; E. Panofsky, *Die Perspektive als symbolische Form, Studien d. Bibliothek Warburg*, 1927, p. 289; P. Halm in *JPKS* 53, 1932, pp. 207 ff.; Becker, no. 17; *Altdorfer-Ausstellung*, no. 123; O. Benesch, *Der Maler Albrecht Altdorfer*, 1939, p. 23; Baldass, 1941, p. 156; Winkler, *Altdeutsche Zeichnungen*, p. 66; Winzinger, no. 110.

This interesting drawing is a preparatory study for the painting entitled the *Birth of Mary, Surrounded by Angels*, now in the Munich Pinakothek. It bears witness to Altdorfer's knowledge of perspective, although the construction is not carried out logically throughout. Altdorfer as draftsman and painter obviously aspired to a representation of architectural space that was more pictorial than architectonic. A group of architectural drawings, discovered by Peter Halm in the Wolfegg collection, are close to the Berlin work.

No one has been able so far to attribute these drawings to Altdorfer with any degree of certainty. In the Berlin *Church Interior* gothic elements mingle with Italian Renaissance forms. It is probable that Altdorfer was inspired by the designs for the pilgrimage church of the *Schöne Maria* in Regensburg (see cat. 130), whose construction was begun in 1519 after the destruction of the synagogue. This drawing, a copy of which is also in the Leipzig Museum, can thus be dated in the vicinity of 1520-25.

ERHARD ALTDORFER

Painter, engraver, designer of woodcuts, and architect. Seems to have been born shortly after 1480 in Regensburg. Active from 1512 until his death in 1561 in Mecklenburg as court painter.

133. *Banqueters at a Fountain*

Pen and black ink. 148 x 222 mm, 5⅞ x 8¾ in. In an unknown hand above: 1506.

Coll. King Friedrich-Wilhelm I (Lugt 1631). KdZ 85.

BIBLIOGRAPHY: Friedländer, 1891, no. 2; Voss, *Donaustil*, p. 197; Lippmann-Grote, 2nd ed., no. 188; Friedländer-Bock, p. 4; L. Baldass, 1923, p. 30; H. Hildebrandt, *Die Architektur bei Altdorfer*, 1908, p. 53; Becker, no. 85 and p. 88; *Altdorfer-Ausstellung*, no. 68; L. Baldass in *JKSW* 12, 1938, p. 117; C. Koch in *ZKG* 7, 1938, p. 225; Baldass, 1941, p. 222; Winzinger, no. 145; Oettinger, *Datum und Signatur*, p. 65; Id., *Altdorfer-Studien*, pp. 82 ff.; O. Benesch and E. Auer, *Die Historia Friderici et Maximiliani*, 1957, pp. 85 ff.; K. Arndt in *Kunstchronik* 11, 1958, p. 228; F. Winzinger in *B M* 13, 1963, p. 27.

Close as it is to Albrecht Altdorfer, this drawing could not be taken for his work because of the relative lifelessness of the line. Hanna Weber was the first to recognize the presence of another hand. Connoisseurs such as C. Dodgson, B. Shaw, and O. Benesch expressed their agreement with an attribution to Erhard Altdorfer on the occasion of the large Altdorfer Exhibition in 1938 (*Altdorfer-Ausstellung*, 2nd ed., no. 68). This attribution has since then come to be generally accepted and thoroughly confirmed by the two engravings *Lover Accompanied by Two Girls* (H.3) and *Lady with Peacock Coat of Arms* (H.1). The date of 1506, added later at the upper edge in early sixteenth-century style, is confirmed as correct because of the date that appears on the engraving of the peacock arms.

This drawing is the key to the early work of Erhard, who was only slightly younger than his brother, the more important artist of the two and the one who largely influenced Erhard's artistic formation. The differences between their respective qualities are, however, easily discernible. Erhard still hides his ignorance of human anatomy under the weight of ponderous garments. Figures such as the walking knight, at the right of this drawing, reveal that the young artist was also influenced by the engravings of Master MZ (Matthäus Zasinger, see cat. 115). The finesse and care lavished upon the linear execution of this drawing clearly show Erhard's interest in engraving.

MASTER OF THE *HISTORIA FRIDERICI ET MAXIMILIANI* (PULKAU MASTER)

Painter and draftsman in the circle of Albrecht Altdorfer. Probably active in Vienna between 1510 and 1520.

134. *Chivalric Scene*

Pen and black ink, heightened with white on brown tinted paper. 215 x 163 mm, 8½ x 6⅜ in. Strip in the upper part probably added by the artist. Dated above: 1514.

Coll. v. Nagler (Lugt 2529). Acquired 1835. KdZ 93.

BIBLIOGRAPHY: M. J. Friedländer, *A. Altdorfer, der Maler von Regensburg*, 1891, no. 7; Voss, *Donaustil*, pp. 148 and 197; Friedländer, p. 5; L. Baldass, *A. Altdorfer*, 1923, p. 69; M. J. Friedländer, 1923, no. 66; H. L. Becker, *Die Handzeichnungen A. Altdorfers*, 1938, no. 86; B. Kurth in *GK* n.s. 3, 1938, pp. 2 ff.; *Altdorfer-Ausstellung*, no. 103; F. Winzinger, *Altdorfer Zeichnungen*, 1952, no. 139; K.

Oettinger, *Datum und Signatur bei W. Huber u. A. Altdorfer*, 1957, p. 61; Id., *Altdorfer-Studien*, 1959, p. 118; O. Benesch-E. Auer, *Die Historia Friderici et Maximiliani*, 1957, p. 130, no. 15.

This anonymous artist takes his name from the drawing in pen and ink with water-color made to illustrate the *Historia Friderici et Maximiliani* (Vienna, Haus- Hof- and Staatarchiv, Ms. Böhm no. 24), edited by Joseph Grünpeck. His masterpiece in painting is the central altarpiece for the Church of the Holy Blood in Pulkau (Lower Austria). As early as 1907 H. Voss had grouped these illustrations under the denomination of the Master of the Confused Drawing Style, together with a series of drawings among which were, notably, the drawing pictured here and one by Erhard Altdorfer (cat. 133). However, he later attributed them to Master MZ (Matthäus Zasinger). Benesch was the first to draw attention to the relationship between the illustrations and the Pulkau paintings (*JKSW*, n.s. 2, 1928, pp. 117 ff.; *Belvedere* 9, 1939-II, p. 81; *Österreichische Handzeichnungen des 15. und 16. Jahrhunderts, Die Meisterzeichnung* 5, 1936, pp. 51 ff.). He nonetheless distinguishes between authentic drawings and those which are simply the result of an attribution in the catalogue of other works by the Master of the *Historia*. This catalogue is part of the book which he devoted to this Master (pp. 129 ff.). This distinction, however, seems rather arbitrary, since apart from the illustrations for the *Historia* the classification of all other works grouped under the name of this artist rest upon attributions. Oettinger and Winzinger quite rightly place these drawings in the category of acknowledged works by this Master.

The artist's style is related to that of Albrecht Altdorfer in the years 1506-08. All writers agree that the drawing in question here was based upon a lost original by Albrecht Altdorfer, dating in the vicinity of 1510. The Museum of Fine Arts in Budapest has a somewhat coarser replica or copy of the Berlin drawing. In the extreme delicacy of his draftsmanship this Master is also very close to Erhard's style of the same period.

WOLF HUBER

Painter, designer of woodcuts, architect. Born around 1480-90 in Feldkirch, Vorarlberg (Austria). Died in Passau in 1553 where he held the post of official painter and architect to the Bishop.

BIBLIOGRAPHY: R. Riggenbach, *Der Maler und Zeichner Wolf Huber* (Diss. Basel), 1907; P. Halm in *MJBK*, n.s. 7, 1930, pp. 1 ff.; M. Weinberger, *Wolf Huber*, 1930; *Altdorfer-Ausstellung*; E. Heinzle, *Wolf Huber*.

135. *Landscape with a Fortress*

Pen and brown ink. 191 x 130 mm, 7½ x 5⅛ in.

Part of the original collection. KdZ 97.

BIBLIOGRAPHY: Riggenbach, p. 55, note 1; Friedländer-Bock, pp. 57 and 374; Weinberger, pp. 33 ff.; Halm, no. 3; *Altdorfer-Ausstellung*, no. 447; Heinzle, no. 3; K. Oettinger in *JKSW* 53, n.s. 17, 1957, p. 90.

As early as the supplement to the Berlin catalogue (p. 374), its authors had corrected Riggenbach's dating which had read "*after* 1520." And indeed, the Berlin drawing belongs to Huber's first period. Today the work is believed to have been executed between 1511 and 1513. As opposed to the very well-known drawing of the *Mondsee with the Schafberg* of 1510 (Nuremberg, Germanisches Nationalmuseum), we are confronted here, as Halm has shown, with an imaginary landscape containing elements borrowed from the landscapes of Pacher.

136. *Crucifixion*

Pen and brown ink. 203 x 152 mm, 8 x 6⅜ in. Signed below on the stone and dated 1517.

Coll. Strauss. Acquired 1906. KdZ 4325.

BIBLIOGRAPHY: *Blätter für Gemäldekunde* 3, 1906; Lippmann-Grote, 2nd ed., no. 192; Springer, *Federzeichnungen*, pl. 12; Riggenbach, p. 36; Weinberger, pp. 83 and 98; Friedländer-Bock, p. 56; Halm, no. 5; Heinzle, no. 35; Oettinger, *Datum und Signatur bei W. Huber und A. Altdorfer*, 1957, no. 17; K. Oettinger in *JKSW* 53 (n.s. 17), 1957, pp. 71 ff.

In the years 1515-22 Huber was concerned with representing the human figure within a landscape. Initially all the importance is centered upon the figure, with the landscape used only as a background. In the *Crucifixion*, however, an equilibrium is established among the figure, landscape, and space. The figures openly dominate the composition without overpowering it. There is a marked differentiation in the rendering of the various parts of the drawing: the foreground is treated with great forcefulness, whereas the background is handled in a more delicate manner.

137. *Lower Alpine Landscape*

Pen and ink, heightened with gouache and watercolor. 211 x 306 mm, 8⅜ x 12 in. Signed below: W.H.; dated above, 1532.

Coll. Pacetti (Lugt 2057). Acquired 1844. KdZ 2061.

BIBLIOGRAPHY: Lichtenberg, *Zur Entwicklungsgeschichte der Landschaftsmalerei d. Deutschen und Niederländer im 16. Jahrhundert*, 1892, pp. 108 ff.; Riggenbach, p. 54, note 2; Friedländer-Bock, p. 56; Weinberger, p. 100; Halm, no. 6; *Altdorfer-Ausstellung*, no. 474; Heinzle, no. 91.

P. Halm and E. Buchner are agreed (in the catalogue of the Altdorfer exhibition) that the third numeral of the date, the "2," had been later transformed into a "3." The colored landscape drawing, formerly in the Königs Collection, Rotterdam, is also dated 1522. These two signed and dated pages and a third watercolor, now in Erlangen, form a small group within Huber's oeuvre. The two Berlin drawings cannot be considered studies, but rather drawings conceived as definitive works on the order of those of Altdorfer. No one has as yet attempted to identify the landscape, and in fact it is even questionable whether Huber had a specific place in mind.

138. *Bust of a Beardless Man Wearing a Cap*

Charcoal, heightened with white on tinted brick-red paper. 275 x 201 mm, 10⅞ x 7⅞ in. Signed at the right and dated 1522 at the upper left.

Coll. v. Nagler (Lugt 2529). Acquired 1835. KdZ 2060.

BIBLIOGRAPHY: M. J. Friedländer, *A. Altdorfer*, 1891, p. 163, note 72; Voss, *Donaustil*, p. 25; Friedländer-Bock, p. 56; Weinberger, p. 125; *Altdorfer-Ausstellung*, no. 470; Heinzle, no. 80; *Deutsche Zeichnungen 1400-1900*, no. 86; *Wolf Huber-Gedächtnis-Ausstellung*, Passau, 1953, no. 53.

Huber made seven studies of heads dated 1522 and executed, for the most part, on tinted brick-red paper. Besides the work in Basel, this drawing should most likely be considered a life study. The strictly frontal representation confers great dignity to this ascetic head. It is tempting to view this drawing as a self-portrait. There is a modified copy of this drawing in the Dresden Print Room (no. C.2131, illus. *Portret Niemiecki 1500-1800*, catalogue of the Warsaw Exhibition, 1961, no. 86, pl. 3, described there as a self-portrait).

139. *The Transfiguration*

Pen and ink with wash. 191 x 150 mm, 7½ x 5⅛ in. Signed in the lower center and dated in the clouds, below Christ: 1526. At the upper edge: Matth 7.

Coll. Rodrigues (Lugt 897). Acquired 1921. KdZ 11 732.

BIBLIOGRAPHY: Sale catalogue of the Rodrigues collection, Amsterdam, F. Muller and Co. 12-13, 7, 1921, no. 47; Weinberger, p. 152; Halm, no. 7; Altdorfer exhibition, no. 481; Heinzle, no. 106.

Along with other pages related to it by their graphic quality, this work is thought to be a study for a painting. Toward the middle of the 1520's Huber developed a new style. Figures and landscape are reduced to their outlines and barest elaboration within the forms. As shown in this *Transfiguration*, the new style included the addition of a final wash.

140. *View of a City with a Large Bridge*

Pen and ink with wash. 228 x 310 mm, 9 x 12¼ in. Dated above 1542.

Coll. Campe (Lugt 1391). Acquired 1917. KdZ 8496.

BIBLIOGRAPHY: M. J. Friedländer, *Von Schongauer bis Holbein, d. J.*, pl. 27; Friedländer-Bock, *Handzeichnungen*, pl. 65; Friedländer-Bock, pp. 56 and 374; Weinberger, p. 190; Halm, no. 10; *Altdorfer-Ausstellung*, no. 499; Heinzle, no. 159.

This drawing, which achieves its extraordinary effect through the dramatic formation of the sky and the sweeping curve of the bridge in the foreground, does not seem to represent an actual place. Certain elements such as the situation of the water and the dominant position of the church are reminiscent of the city of Passau, the city where Huber worked. The rather summary treatment of the sky, as well as other superficial aspects of the drawing, have caused Halm to doubt its authenticity. However, the precise rendering of the buildings still argues in favor of a Huber attribution. No other master of the Danube School other than Huber would have been capable at that time of so richly inventive a city view.

MONOGRAMMIST HF (HANS FRANCK)

The monogrammist HF can probably be identified with the painter Hans Franck, mentioned between 1505 and 1510 in the Basel archives.

141. *Witches' Sabbath*

Pen and black ink, heightened with white on gray tinted paper. 143 x 104 mm, 5⅝ x 4⅛ in. Signed HF and dated 1515 at the upper left.

Coll. v. Lanna. Acquired 1910. KdZ 4454.

BIBLIOGRAPHY: Schönbrunner-Meder, no. 1186; Friedländer-Bock, p. 43; M. Grünwald in *JPKS* 44, 1923, pp. 30 ff.; Baldung-Grien, 2nd ed., no. 316.

This drawing and several others signed in the same way are by the hand of the same artist who executed a series of woodcuts for Strasburg and Basel printers, all bearing the same inscription: H.F. As early as 1898 Schmid had proposed that the monogrammist H.F. could be identfed with the painter Hans Franck mentioned in the Basel archives. The works of this artist show his close affinity to Hans Baldung. This scene of a Witches' Sabbath, moreover, was probably inspired by varying representations of the same scene by Baldung. On the other hand, the works of H.F. contain features which would indicate a familiarity with the art of the Danube School.

ANONYMOUS MASTER, ca. 1500

142. *Pairs of Lovers in a Hall*

Pen and black ink, washed with gray and opaque white. 203 x 311 mm, 8 x 12¼ in. Inscribed below, in the seventeenth century: Johan Balden Grün f.

Coll. King Friedrich-Wilhelm I (Lugt 1631). KdZ 1412.

BIBLIOGRAPHY: Lippmann-Grote, 1st ed., no. 36, 2nd ed., no. 164; G. v. Térey, *Die Handzeichnungen des Hans Baldung, gen. Grien*, vol. 1, no. 47, 3rd vol., p. 97; Friedländer-Bock, p. 11.

The attribution of this drawing to Baldung was early rejected by Térey. The costumes of the people in this interesting scene, depicting the customs of the time, date from the beginning of the sixteenth century. The architecture, with its vaulted wooden ceiling and bay window in the center, is typical of the region around Lake Constance, or northern Switzerland.

URS GRAF

Goldsmith, minter of coins, engraver, etcher, designer of woodcuts and windows, mercenary. Born in Solothurn in 1485, active in Strasburg and Basel, where he died in 1527-28.

BIBLIOGRAPHY: K. T. Parker in *ASAK*, n.s. 23, 1921, pp. 207 ff.; H. Koegler, *Beschreibendes Verzeichnis der Basler Handzeichnungen des Urs Graf* (published jointly as a catalogue at the Urs Graf exhibition, 1926); W. Lüthi, *Urs Graf und die Kunst der alten Schweizer*, 1928.

143. *Design for a Dagger Sheath with St. George*

Pen and black ink. 263 x 28 mm, 10⅜ x 1⅛ in.

Coll. P. Davidsohn (Lugt 654). Acquired 1916. KdZ 8461.

BIBLIOGRAPHY: Friedländer-Bock, p. 44; Parker, no. 8; Lüthi, no. 206.

Aside from four designs for daggers and knives in Basel, the Berlin drawing is the only preparatory study for metalwork designed by Urs Graf. As is shown in a niello proof of a sword scabbard, of which half is in Berlin and the other half in Basel, such designs were meant to be engraved (E. Major-E. Gradmann, *Urs Graf*, pls. 88-89). These studies for metalwork are generally dated around the years 1511-12.

144. *Adoration of the Magi*

Pen and India ink. Watermark: crown (Briquet 4673). 312 x 203 mm, 12¼ x 8 in. Signed with monogram on a plaque at the upper right and dated 151[3]. Second monogram at the lower left.

Coll. Hausmann (Lugt 377). Acquired 1875. KdZ 396.

BIBLIOGRAPHY: Lippmann-Grote, 2nd ed., no. 196; Friedländer-Bock, p. 44; Parker, no. 5; Lüthi, no. 162.

Although this page has been cut down on all sides, the composition has lost nothing of its force and value. As opposed to his contemporaries, Urs Graf reserved only a minor part of his work for religious subjects. When he did treat these themes, his savagery of line and composition frequently approach the blasphemous. This *Adoration*, however, does not lack the religious dignity appropriate to the subject.

145. *Peasant Couple Dancing*

Pen and black ink. 211 x 157 mm, 8⅜ x 6⅛ in. Signed with monogram below and dated 1525.

Coll. J. C. Robinson (Lugt 1433). Acquired 1902. KdZ 4243.

BIBLIOGRAPHY: Ganz, *Handzeichnungen* III, 48; Friedländer-Bock, p. 44; Parker, no. 7; Koegler, no. 139; Lüthi, no. 161.

In 1525 Urs Graf portrayed scenes of dancing peasants and musicians in a series of drawings. (Eleven are known to have survived and are now scattered in different collections.) He thus utilized a theme that, since Dürer, had been favored by German graphic art and that Sebald Beham, for example, had treated in a series of small engravings. Graf probably did not originate his physical types, although their direct model has not yet been found. Koegler believes (no. 118) that the idea was suggested to him by the frieze of dancing peasants depicted on the "Haus zum Tanz" in Basel (see cat. 109). The great care which Graf lavished on these groups leads us to suppose that he intended using them for woodcuts. The outlines of a few of the drawings have been pricked with a needle, indicating eventual transfer to the wood block.

NIKLAUS MANUEL DEUTSCH

Painter and designer of woodcuts, poet, politician, and mercenary. Born in 1484 in Bern, where he died in 1530.

> BIBLIOGRAPHY: B. Haendcke, *Niklaus Manuel Deutsch als Künstler*, 1889; L. Stumm, *Niklaus Manuel Deutsch von Bern als bildender Künstler*, 1925; H. Koegler, *Beschreibendes Verzeichnis der Basler Handzeichnungen des Niklaus Manuel Deutsch* (published jointly as a catalogue of the Basel exhibition of Niklaus Manuel Deutsch at the Print Room, 1930); W. Hugelshofer, *Schweizer Handzeichnungen des 15. und 16. Jahrhunderts, Die Meisterzeichnung*, 1, 1928; C. von Mandach-H. Koegler, *Niklaus Manuel Deutsch*.

146. *Martyrdom of Holy Knights*

> Pen and black ink on parchment. 510 x 620 mm, 20⅛ x 24½ in. Signed at the lower right: NMD.
>
> Given by the Kunstgewerbemuseum (Fine Arts Library), Berlin, in 1915. KdZ 8206.
>
> BIBLIOGRAPHY: Friedländer-Bock, p. 66; Stamm, no. 140; Hugelshofer, no. 18; Koegler, no. 96; Von Mandach-Koegler, p. 43, pl. 67.

This tripartite composition, whose subject is the martyrdom of holy knights, has been interpreted as a design for a choir gate. A working drawing for the gate in the Bern cathedral and Manuel Deutsch's profound knowledge of sculpture prove that the artist was also familiar with many aspects of architectural sculpture. The technicalities of execution are open to discussion; at the very least one wonders whether Manuel had reliefs or free-standing groups in mind. Today we know that, at this period, projects for both sculpture-in-the-round and reliefs were frequently designed by painters (see cat. 38), and it is within this context that Niklaus' drawing should be situated, dated around 1516.

147. *Landscape with Rocks*

Pen and black ink. 257 x 198 mm, 10⅛ x 7⅞ in.

Coll. Archduke Friedrich of Austria (Lugt 960) and Edwin Czeczowiczka. Acquired 1930. KdZ 14 698.

BIBLIOGRAPHY: Schönbrunner-Meder, n.s. 1922, pl. 130; Stumm, no. 1; Hugelshofer, no. 13; Koegler, no. 104.

The attribution of this page to Manuel Deutsch goes back to Meder. A similar drawing, representing a rock in the form of a tower, is in the Basel Print Room. The Berlin work was long considered the preparatory study for the nearly square Basel drawing, which is why it was given a rather early date, between 1512 and 1514. Koegler was probably correct in dating the drawing in the vicinity of 1518, since the greater certainty of line and more centralized perspective clearly argue in favor of this date. The towering rock near a sheet of water is not an actual landscape. Rather, both drawings may be said to resume the dominant elements of the Swiss landscape within a free composition. As opposed to the tradition of the German provinces, the landscape as genre had only minor significance in Switzerland. Even Manuel Deutsch rarely treated landscape as an independent subject. The lower edge, bearing the monogram, was probably cut off.

148. *One of the Five Wise Virgins*

Pen and black ink, heightened with white on reddish-brown tinted paper. 290 x 192 mm, 11⅜ x 7⅞ in. Signed with monogram and interlaced dagger at the lower left.

Coll. WHJ. v. Nagler (Lugt 2529). Acquired 1835. KdZ 877.

BIBLIOGRAPHY: Haendcke, p. 47; Friedländer-Bock, p. 66; Stumm, no. 48; Koegler, no. 101.

This drawing constitutes the later development of the motif of a charcoal drawing in Basel, which belongs to the series of the *Foolish Virgins* (Koegler no. 20). From the stylistic point of view it also constitutes a transition toward the woodcut series of 1518, although the same motif does not re-emerge there. In technique this page goes back to the end of 1517 or the beginning of 1518.

149. *Standing Witch*

Pen and black ink with wash and heightened with white on red tinted paper. 276 x 143 mm, 10⅞ x 5⅝ in. Signed with monogram and dagger.

Acquired 1917. KdZ 8480.

BIBLIOGRAPHY: *BM* 38, 1916-17, p. 181; Friedländer-Bock, p. 66; Stumm, no. 77; Koegler, no. 103; Von Mandach-Koegler, 44, pl. 79.

The force of the facial expression and balanced play of limbs make this page one of the most extraordinary of Manuel Deutsch's works. In the years 1515 and 1516 the painter drew a remarkable series of female nudes, within which Koegler places this drawing of a witch. He nonetheless dates it in the beginning of 1518, as the chiaroscuro technique already points to a later phase of Manuel Deutsch's style.

150. *The Virgin with the Infant Christ, Seated at the Base of a Column*

Pen and black ink, heightened with white on red tinted paper. 310 x 210 mm, 12 ¼ x 8 ¼ in. Signed with monogram and dagger at the lower right.

Coll. v. Nagler (Lugt 2529). Acquired 1835. KdZ 1378.

BIBLIOGRAPHY: Woltmann-Woerman, *Kunstgeschichte*, vol. 3, 1882, p. 485; Haendcke, p. 80, no. 135; Schneeli, *Renaissance in der Schweiz*, pl. XI and p. 93; Lippmann-Grote, 1st ed., no. 78; 2nd ed., no. 195; Brun, *Schweizerisches Künstlerlexikon;* Friedländer-Bock, p. 65; Stumm, no. 86; Koegler, no. 112; Von Mandach-Koegler, pl. 99; Winkler, *Altdeutsche Zeichnungen*, p. 55.

Koegler considers this work to be the best drawing by Manuel Deutsch. He quite rightly draws our attention to the formal and technical relationship between this work and the drawing on the same theme by Holbein the Younger showing the *Holy Family* (Basel). While this work is generally dated between 1516 and 1521 Koegler, basing his conclusion on this relationship, arrives at a later date, no earlier than 1522.

Illustrations

1. MARTIN SCHONGAUER: St. Dorothy, Seated

2. MARTIN SCHONGAUER: Bust of an Old Man Wearing Fur Collar and Fur Hat

3. SCHOOL OF MARTIN SCHONGAUER: St. Margaret

4. SCHOOL OF MARTIN SCHONGAUER: St. Dorothy

5. NUREMBERG MASTER, CA. 1480: Study of a Woman

6. NUREMBERG MASTER: The Baptism of Christ

7. THE HOUSEBOOK MASTER: A Prince at Table

8. THE HOUSEBOOK MASTER: Three Men in Conversation

9. MASTER OF THE STÖTTERITZ ALTAR: Study for a Triptych

10. MICHAEL WOLGEMUT: Group of Five Standing Men

11. VEIT STOSS: Presentation at the Temple

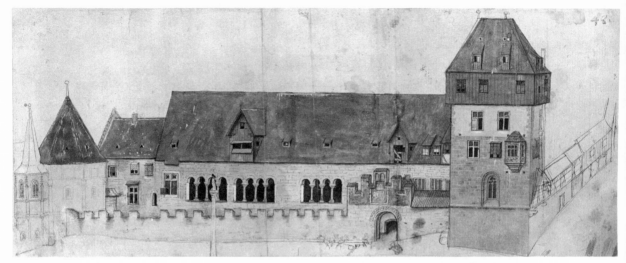

12. WOLFGANG KATZHEIMER: The Imperial and Episcopal Palace, Bamberg

13. WOLFGANG KATZHEIMER: The "Court of the Burgraves," Bamberg

14. WOLFGANG KATZHEIMER: Above: Curia Buildings of the Cathedral, Bamberg
Below: The Cloister of Michelsberg, Bamberg

15. MASTER OF THE DRAPERY STUDIES: Studies for an Entombment or a Lamentation

16. MONOGRAMMIST MFP OF 1495: Five Pairs of Fencers

17. ALBRECHT DÜRER: Virgin Enthroned with the Infant Christ

18. ALBRECHT DÜRER: Three Lansquenets

19. ALBRECHT DÜRER: Couple on Horseback

20. ALBRECHT DÜRER: St. Catherine

21. ALBRECHT DÜRER: The Quarry

22. ALBRECHT DÜRER: Valley near Kalchreuth

23. ALBRECHT DÜRER: *Angel Playing a Lute*

24. ALBRECHT DÜRER: Male Nude Fighting a Dragon

25. ALBRECHT DÜRER: Faun

26. ALBRECHT DÜRER: Three Peasants and a Peasant Couple

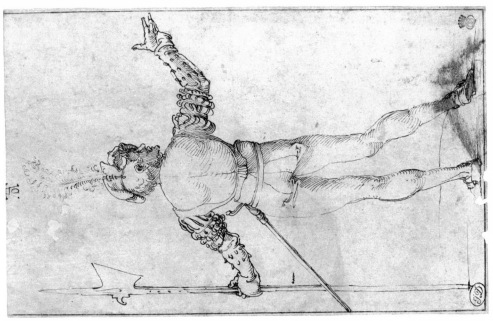

28. ALBRECHT DÜRER: Lansquenet Seen from the Back

27. ALBRECHT DÜRER: Forest Spring with St. Paul and St. Anthony

29. ALBRECHT DÜRER: Portrait of Willibald Pirckheimer

1503·

30. ALBRECHT DÜRER: Profile Portrait of Willibald Pirckheimer

31. ALBRECHT DÜRER: Annunciation

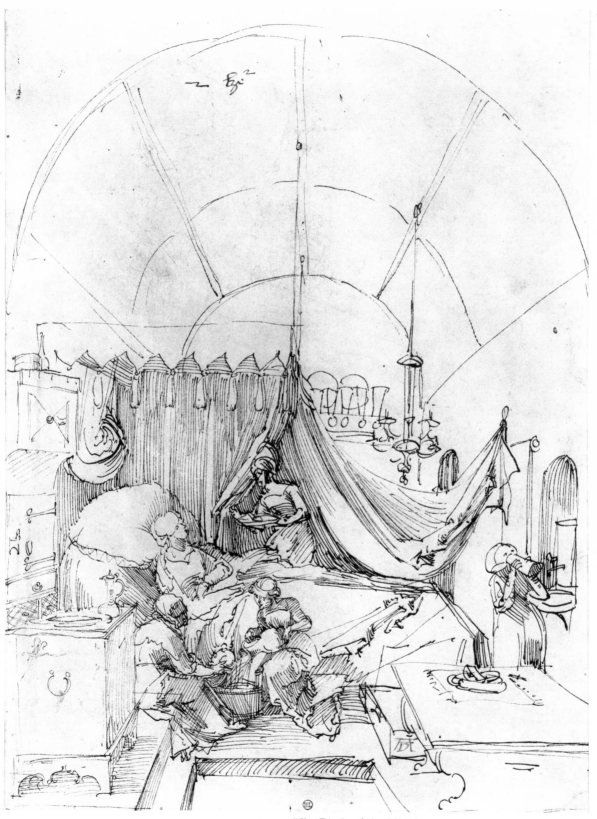

32. ALBRECHT DÜRER: The Birth of the Virgin

33. ALBRECHT DÜRER: The Arrest of Christ

34. ALBRECHT DÜRER: Drapery Studies

35. ALBRECHT DÜRER: Portrait of an Architect

36. ALBRECHT DÜRER: Female Nude with a Shield

37. ALBRECHT DÜRER: Kneeling Apostle

38. ALBRECHT DÜRER: Samson Conquering the Philistines

39. ALBRECHT DÜRER: The Rest on the Flight into Egypt

40. ALBRECHT DÜRER: Virgin and Child on a Crescent Moon

41. ALBRECHT DÜRER: Portrait of a Young Girl

42. ALBRECHT DÜRER: St. Catherine, Seated

43. ALBRECHT DÜRER: Woman Seated on a Bench

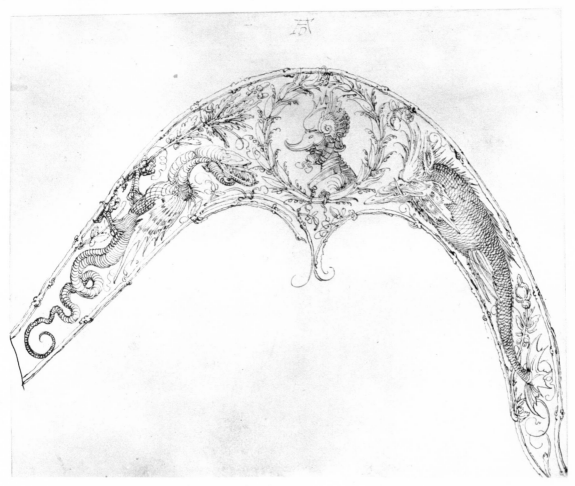

44. ALBRECHT DÜRER: Ornament for Armor

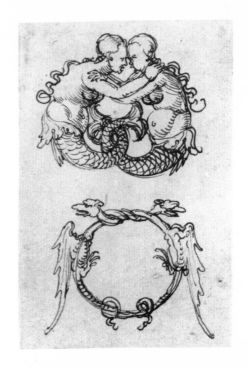

45. ALBRECHT DÜRER: Two Designs for Jewelry

47. ALBRECHT DÜRER: Portrait of Paul Topler and Martin Pfinzing

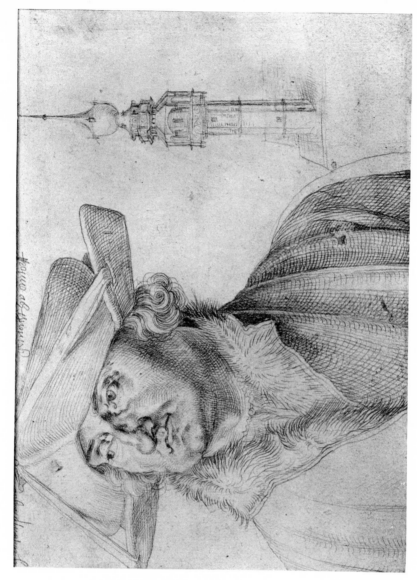

48. ALBRECHT DÜRER: Portrait of Lazarus Ravensburger

46. ALBRECHT DÜRER: Portrait of a Mechelen Goldsmith

49. ALBRECHT DÜRER: Head of an Old Man

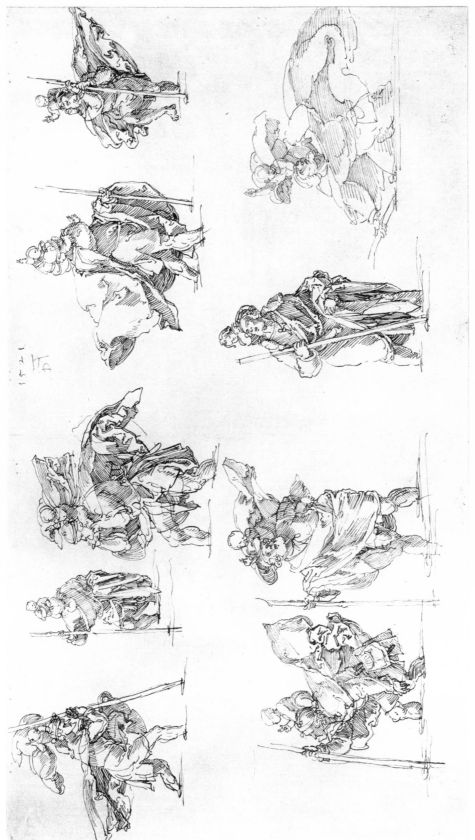

50. ALBRECHT DÜRER: Study Sheet for a St. Christopher

51. ALBRECHT DÜRER: Portrait of a Young Man

52. ALBRECHT DÜRER: Irish Soldiers and Peasants

53. ALBRECHT DÜRER: St. Apollonia

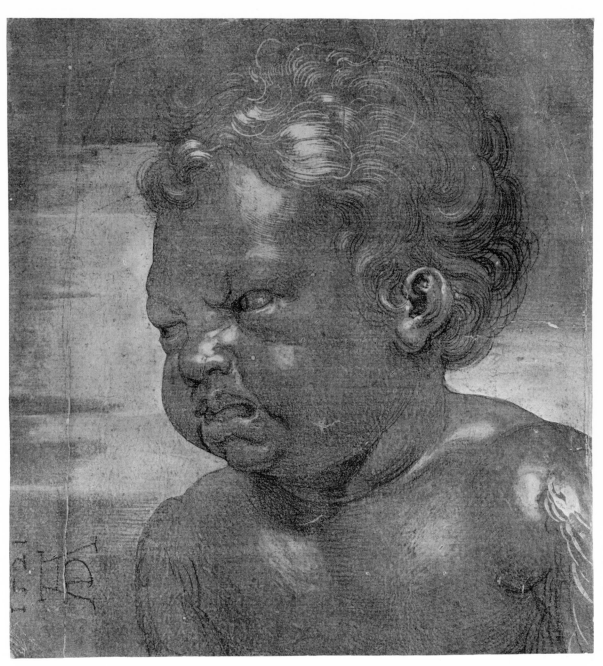

54. ALBRECHT DÜRER: Weeping Angel

55. ALBRECHT DÜRER: Head of St. Mark

56. ALBRECHT DÜRER: Group for a Bearing of the Cross

57. PETER VISCHER THE YOUNGER: Virtutes et Voluptas

58. PETER VISCHER THE YOUNGER: The Dream of Hercules

59. GRÜNEWALD: Kneeling Figure with Two Angels

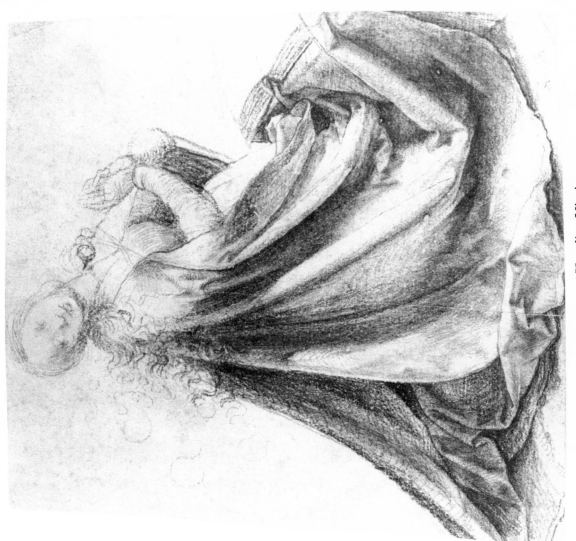

60. GRÜNEWALD: Kneeling Virgin

61. GRÜNEWALD: Recto: Head of a Singing Angel

62. GRÜNEWALD: Verso: Study for the Head of a Young Woman

63. LUCAS CRANACH THE ELDER: A Thief on the Cross

64. LUCAS CRANACH THE ELDER: A Thief on the Cross

65. LUCAS CRANACH THE ELDER: Lucretia

66. LUCAS CRANACH THE ELDER: Boar and Dogs

67. LUCAS CRANACH THE ELDER: Portrait of a Beardless Man

68. LUCAS CRANACH THE ELDER: Project for a Polyptych

68. A.) St. Titus (outer wings when closed)

68. B.) St. Mark, St. Andrew, St. Timothy (inner panels when closed)

69. LUCAS CRANACH THE YOUNGER: Portrait of a Man with a Beard

70. HANS SÜSS VON KULMBACH: Three Studies of Women's Costumes

71. HANS SÜSS VON KULMBACH: Portrait of Abbot Johannes Rottenecker

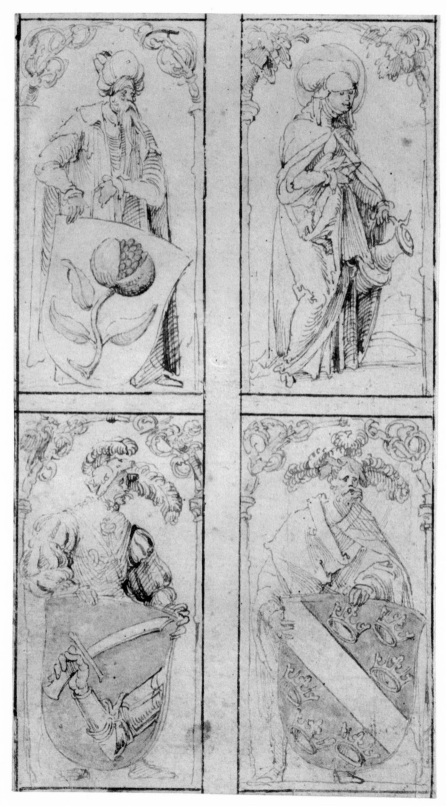

72. HANS SÜSS VON KULMBACH: Design for a Window

73. HANS SÜSS VON KULMBACH: The Annunciation

74. HANS SCHÄUFELEIN: The Nativity

75. HANS SCHÄUFELEIN: Lady Wearing a Headdress

76. HANS SCHÄUFELEIN: Portrait of a Man

77. BARTHEL BEHAM: Moses Rescued from the Bulrushes

78. HANS SEBALD BEHAM: The Massacre of the Innocents

79. LEONHARD BECK: Portrait of Count Moritz von Ertingen

80. PETER FLÖTNER: Design for a Ceremonial Chair

81. PETER FLÖTNER: Design for a Dagger

82. AUGUSTIN HIRSCHVOGEL: The Castle of Neuburg on the Danube

83. HANS BALDUNG GRIEN: The Beheading of St. Barbara

84. HANS BALDUNG GRIEN: Seated Witch

85. HANS BALDUNG GRIEN: Drunken Bacchus

86. HANS BALDUNG GRIEN: A Lady at Prayer

87. HANS BALDUNG GRIEN:
   Portrait of a Burgher's Wife

88. HANS BALDUNG GRIEN:
   Young Girl Wearing a Necklace

89. HANS BALDUNG GRIEN: Venus with an Apple

90. HANS BALDUNG GRIEN: Masquerade Before a Castle

1 5 3 4

91. HANS BALDUNG GRIEN: Sketch for a Window

92. HANS LEU: The Rest on the Flight into Egypt

93. HEINRICH ALDEGREVER: Portrait of a Man

94. BERNHARD STRIGEL: Doubting Thomas

95. HANS HOLBEIN THE ELDER: The Martyrdom of St. Paul

Verso: The Duke's Hand Holding the Falcon

96. HANS HOLBEIN THE ELDER: Duke Charles of Burgundy
as a Child (Charles V)

97. HANS HOLBEIN THE ELDER: Portrait of Jakob Fugger

98. HANS HOLBEIN THE ELDER: The Emperor Maximilian
on Horseback

100. HANS HOLBEIN THE ELDER: The Artist's Sons, Ambrosius and Hans

99. HANS HOLBEIN THE ELDER: Portrait of Kunz von der Rosen

102. HANS HOLBEIN THE ELDER: Portrait of Leonhard Wagner

101. HANS HOLBEIN THE ELDER: Portrait of Sigmund Holbein

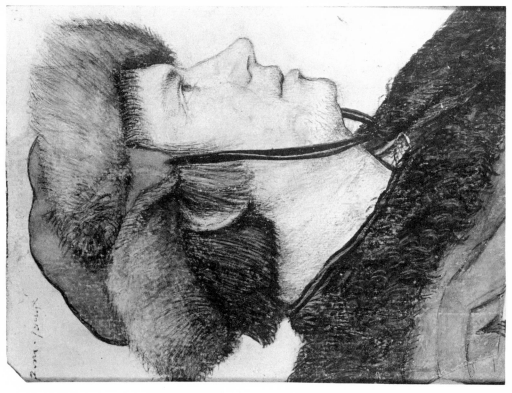

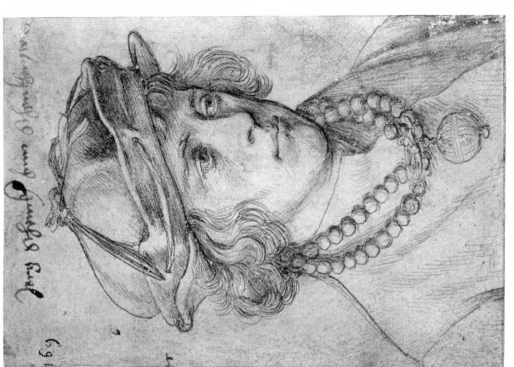

103. HANS HOLBEIN THE ELDER: Portrait of Jörg Schenck zum Schenkenstein   104. HANS HOLBEIN THE ELDER: Portrait of Jörg Bomheckel

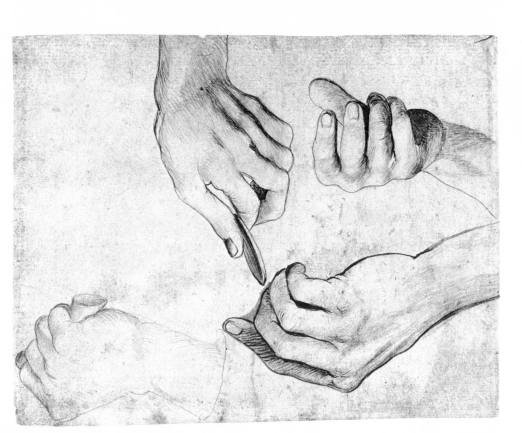

109. HANS HOLBEIN THE YOUNGER: Project of the Fresco Decoration of the
"Haus zum Tanz," Basel

110. HANS HOLBEIN THE YOUNGER: Two Lansquenets Bearing an Escutcheon

III. HANS HOLBEIN THE YOUNGER: Parnassus

112. HANS BURGKMAIR THE ELDER: Christ on the Mount of Olives

113. HANS BURGKMAIR THE ELDER: Study Sheet of Horses' Heads and Harnesses

115. MATTHÄUS ZASINGER:
Two Knights on Horseback

116. SOUTH GERMAN MASTER, CA. 1520: The Virgin on a Crescent Moon

117. JÖRG BREU THE ELDER: Head of a Young Girl

118. JÖRG BREU THE ELDER: Series of the Months: July

119. JÖRG BREU THE ELDER: Series of the Months: October

120. MONOGRAMMIST BB: Portrait of Jörg Lutz

122. MONOGRAMMIST IZ: Portrait of a Young Boy

121. MONOGRAMMIST BB: Portrait of an Unknown Man

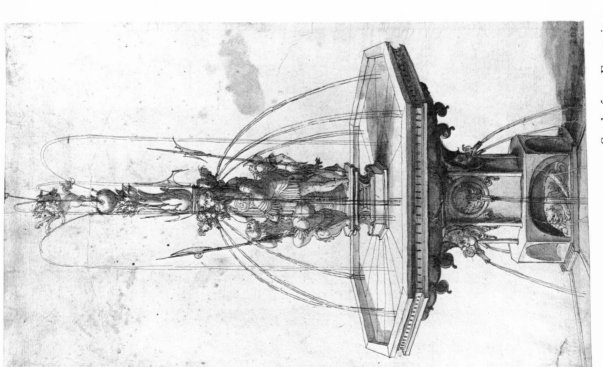

125. DANIEL HOPFER: Tabernacle for the Holy Sacrament

123. SOUTH GERMAN MASTER, CA. 1530: Study for a Fountain

126. ALBRECHT ALTDORFER: Landscape with a Pair of Lovers

127. ALBRECHT ALTDORFER: Two Women with a Basket of Fruit

128. ALBRECHT ALTDORFER: St. Margaret Standing upon the Devil

129. ALBRECHT ALTDORFER: Samson Vanquishing the Lion

130. ALBRECHT ALTDORFER: The Virgin on a Crescent Moon

131. ALBRECHT ALTDORFER: Landscape with a Large Pine

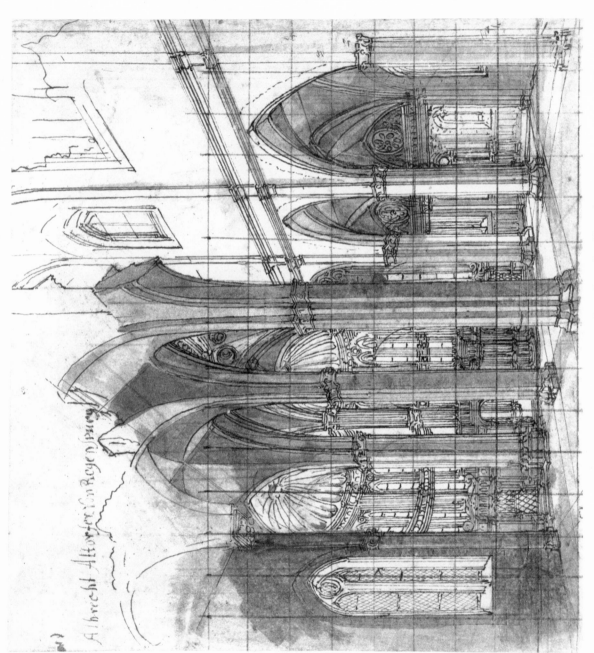

132. ALBRECHT ALTDORFER: Interior of a Church

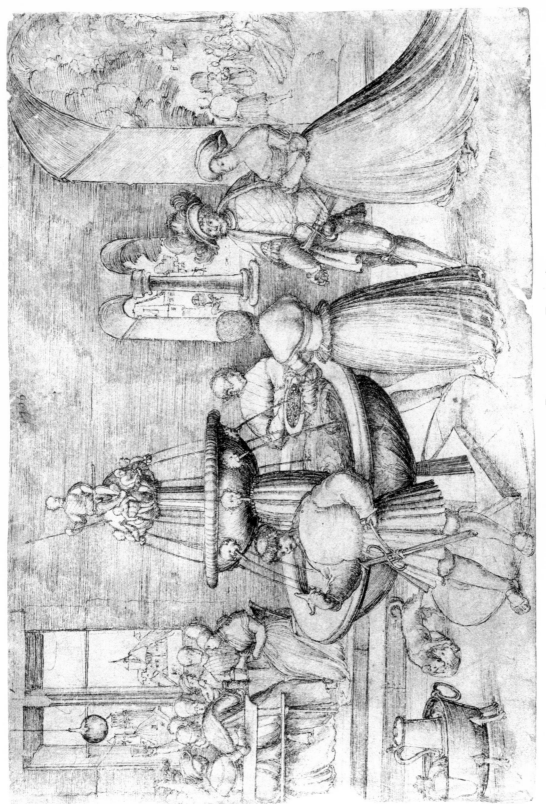

133. ERHARD ALTDORFER: Banqueters at a Fountain

134. MASTER OF THE HISTORIA: Chivalric Scene

135. WOLF HUBER: Landscape with a Fortress

136. WOLF HUBER: Crucifixion: *see frontispiece*

137. WOLF HUBER: Lower Alpine Landscape

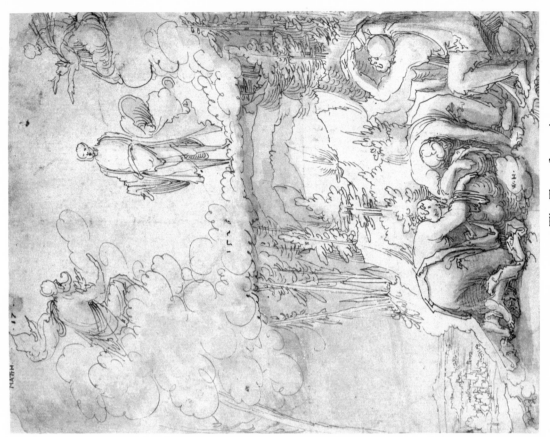

139. WOLF HUBER: The Transfiguration

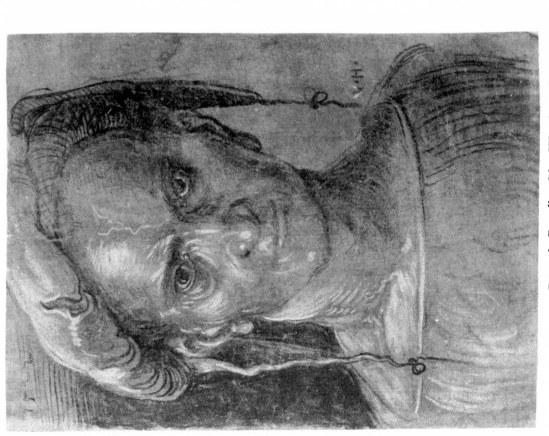

138. WOLF HUBER: Bust of a Beardless Man Wearing a Cap

140. WOLF HUBER: View of a City with a Large Bridge

142. ANONYMOUS MASTER, CA. 1500: Pairs of Lovers in a Hall

141. MONOGRAMMIST HF: Witches' Sabbath

143. URS GRAF: Design for a Dagger Sheath with St. George

144. URS GRAF: Adoration of the Magi

145. URS GRAF: Peasant Couple Dancing

146. NIKLAUS MANUEL DEUTSCH: Martyrdom of Holy Knights

147. NIKLAUS MANUEL DEUTSCH: Landscape with Rocks

148. NIKLAUS MANUEL DEUTSCH: One of the Five Wise Virgins

149. NIKLAUS MANUEL DEUTSCH: Standing Witch

150. NIKLAUS MANUEL DEUTSCH: The Virgin with the Infant Christ

Index of Artists